Diversion Books
A Division of Diversion Publishing Corp.
443 Park Avenue South, Suite 1008
New York, New York 10016
www.DiversionBooks.com

For more information, email info@diversionbooks.com

First Diversion Books edition September 2014.
Print ISBN: 978-1-62681-427-1
eBook ISBN: 978-1-62681-399-1

JUST THE FACTS

THE FIRST STEP IN BUILDING A
NATIONAL STRATEGIC AGENDA FOR AMERICA

NO LABELS FOUNDATION

DIVERSIONBOOKS

CONTENTS

NO LABELS' NATIONAL STRATEGIC AGENDA

The Right Idea at the Right Time

If you wanted to distill the dysfunction in Washington down to one simple phrase, you could do a lot worse than this:

"All tactics, no strategy."

In Congress, there are plenty of hearings being held and laws being proposed.

In government agencies, there are countless programs, initiatives, and imperatives.

What we don't have, as a nation, is any sense of where all of this is taking us.

There are no unifying goals around which a broad cross section of Americans can forge agreement.

No traditional world war we have to win.

No space race we need to lead.

No communist adversary we need to defeat.

In Washington and on the airwaves, we argue about specific policies, laws, and provisions.

But we rarely step back to really think about where we want our nation to go and how we get there.

At No Labels, we believe it's time for America to embrace big goals again.

At the beginning of 2014, No Labels began the process of building a *National Strategic Agenda*, which calls for America's political leaders to commit to a new governing vision that can enable us to:

- Create 25 million new jobs over the next 10 years
- Balance the federal budget by 2030

- Secure Medicare and Social Security for the next 75 years
- Make America energy secure by 2024

No Labels' *National Strategic Agenda* is different than anything that has come before it.

This is not just another policy plan.

In fact, at this point, the *National Strategic Agenda* isn't a policy plan at all, because the specifics of *how* we reach these four signature goals are still to be determined.

In the next year, No Labels is convening meetings with members of Congress; state and local government officials; business and nonprofit leaders; and rank-and-file citizens, to forge agreement on policies that will enable America to meet these goals.

No Labels is taking its politics of problem solving all across the country.

In developing the *National Strategic Agenda*, we aim to bring strategy and long-term vision to a policy-making process that has become too dominated by tactics and short-term political considerations.

This agenda will be developed in a step-by-step fashion that begins with agreement on goals, progresses to agreement on the fundamental facts and concludes with the creation of broad policy principles and specific policy and legislative solutions.

By the fall of 2015, the *National Strategic Agenda* will be a fully developed plan that No Labels will work to make a central point of discussion during the 2016 presidential campaign.

Unlike other plans, the *National Strategic Agenda* won't serve the aims of a particular party or interest group. It will serve the needs and priorities of a broad cross section of Americans, because they'll have a hand in developing it. In fact, the four goals in this agenda were identified by a nationwide survey that No Labels conducted in 2013.

Like everything No Labels has proposed since its launch in December 2010—from our plan to *Make Congress Work!* to our signature "No Budget, No Pay" idea—the *National Strategic Agenda* will be a product of discussion and agreement from every part of the political spectrum.

No Labels believes that if we can forge agreement on a national agenda—based on mutually agreed upon objectives—we can finally start to break the gridlock in our politics today.

Breaking gridlock is a preoccupation and priority of many reform organizations in DC and around the country. Often, these organizations are focused on bold systemic reform ideas to reduce the influence of hyper-partisanship, like getting money out of politics or putting an end to congressional gerrymandering.

These are certainly worthy and important endeavors—but they are tough, multi-year, state-by-state slogs. These ideas may never come to fruition—or only come in time. But America can't afford to wait for the prospect of uncertain reform at some uncertain point in the future.

We need solutions to our most pressing problems *now* and we need buy-in from both Democrats and Republicans to find them.

For too long, partisans on both sides of the aisle have held out for some glorious future where their party has overwhelming control of the White House and Congress and can push through everything they want.

That's not happening anytime soon.

In the meantime, millions of Americans are clamoring for a real plan and real action to deal with our nation's problems.

The *National Strategic Agenda* can be that plan. It deals with issues that are critically important, and interrelated.

For example, fixing Social Security and Medicare makes it a whole lot easier to fix the budget. And creating 25 million new jobs also creates 25 million new taxpayers who can support Social Security and Medicare and help balance our budget.

Meanwhile, producing more affordable, sustainable, and reliable energy—which is the backbone of our economy—will help spur economic growth and job creation and … you guessed it … a more balanced budget.

Meeting any one of the goals in this agenda will make it easier to meet the other ones.

This book that you are about to read will provide a starting point to develop the *National Strategic Agenda* by clarifying a path to its essential goals. In these pages, you will find:

- **Just the Facts:** Before leaders can forge agreement on any issue, they need to be able to agree on the facts. This is surprisingly difficult in Washington, where all sides appear to have their own statistics, baselines, and projections, which often conveniently support whatever policy they are pushing at the moment. This book will cut through the noise to identify the basic facts, trends, and assumptions that must serve as the first step in any serious discussion of these issues.

- **The Urgency:** This book will identify the stakes for each of these four goals—in other words, the bad outcomes that will happen if we don't meet them and the good outcomes that can happen if we do.

- **The History:** We'll explain how we got where we are and how government has tried—and often failed— to deal with these challenges.

- **The Options:** Finally, we will offer a series of principles and policy options that can lead to solutions to all four goals in the *National Strategic Agenda*.

- **The One Imperative That Ties It All Together:** No matter whether you want more or less government, we should all be able to agree that we need smarter, more efficient government. Whatever policy ideas are embraced as part of the *National Strategic Agenda* will only be as effective as the government that has to execute them. So No Labels will also outline a menu of reforms to fix how our government works.

Politicians always tell us that we need to unite our country— but no one ever actually tells us *how* they plan to do it. This book—and this new campaign for a *National Strategic Agenda*— can help provide a road map to a future where good jobs are plentiful, where our seniors can count on Medicare and Social

Security, where our budget is in balance, and where our energy system is secure.

We can do this. Common ground in Washington *does* exist, but our leaders must be empowered to find it. Our leaders can be problem solvers again; they just need a governing vision that brings them together instead of pulling them apart.

This book is a starting point for a great debate to come.

A debate that all Americans need to join.

GOAL #1

CREATE 25 MILLION NEW JOBS OVER THE NEXT 10 YEARS

The Key to Innovation, Prosperity, and the Future

JOB CREATION: JUST THE FACTS

1. Today there are just two job vacancies for every five unemployed Americans actively looking for work.[1][2]

2. The pace of job creation in this recovery has lagged behind that of every other recovery since World War II, signaling a major change in the way our economy functions. No longer do jobs and GDP necessarily rise together.

3. The jobs picture is worse than the unemployment rate indicates. Some 20 million Americans—12.9 percent of the workforce—are either out of work, working fewer hours than they want, or so dejected that they have given up the job hunt altogether.[3][4]

4. The American middle class is no longer the most affluent in the world, and lower-income citizens in Europe earn more than their counterparts here.[5]

SOMETHING HAS CHANGED IN THE U.S. ECONOMY

More than five years after the end of the Great Recession—the most severe economic downturn since the Great Depression—America's economic recovery is a mixed bag.

Gross domestic product is up, as is the stock market. Notwithstanding some concentrated, lingering problems in the housing market, home prices have improved in many parts of

---

1 www.bls.gov/cps/#data
2 www.bls.gov/news.release/jolts.nr0.htm
3 www.bls.gov/lau/stalt.htm
4 www.dlt.ri.gov/lmi/laus/us/usadj.htm
5 www.nytimes.com/2014/04/23/upshot/the-american-middle-class-is-no-longer-the-worlds-richest.html?ref=business&_r=1

the country and normalized in others.[6] Meanwhile, the federal deficit is falling[7] and European economies—not long ago on the verge of collapse—have stabilized.

Most importantly, the 8.7 million jobs the U.S. lost in 2008 and 2009 have been regained.[8]

These developments are welcome. But they aren't enough.

The fact is that America is still stuck in the most sluggish economic recovery of the postwar era.

Today there are just two job vacancies for every five unemployed Americans actively looking for work.[9][10]

The pace of new job creation simply isn't enough to make up for the job hole created by the Great Recession—and the new jobs we are creating aren't as good as the old ones.

Many of these new jobs are in businesses like restaurants, temporary-help firms, and retail outlets—which pay one-half to three-fifths the average hourly wages of construction and manufacturing firms.

Of the jobs lost during the recession, 37 percent were in mid-wage occupations. Of the jobs created during the recovery, only 26 percent have been mid-wage occupations, and 44 percent have been lower wage.[11]

There is no consensus among economists about why this is happening. But there is growing concern that something has fundamentally changed in the American economy.

In modern times, economic recoveries usually followed a predictable pattern:

The economy would grow, and then the jobs would follow.

But starting in the 1990s, job creation after recessions began to lag further and further behind growth.[12] In fact, the aftermath of the two recessions since 2000 have featured a slower pace of job creation than any previous postwar recovery.[13]

6 www.fortune.com/2014/08/04/housing-foreclosures/
7 www.bradenton.com/2014/07/11/5251215/federal-deficit-is-falling-this.html
8 www.latimes.com/business/la-fi-jobs-20140607-story.html
9 www.bls.gov/cps/#data
10 www.bls.gov/news.release/jolts.nr0.htm
11 www.nelp.org/page/-/Reports/Low-Wage-Recovery-Industry-
   Employment-Wages-2014-Report.pdf?nocdn=1
12 www.epi.org/publication/bp259/
13 www.pewresearch.org/fact-tank/2013/09/25/at-42-months-and-

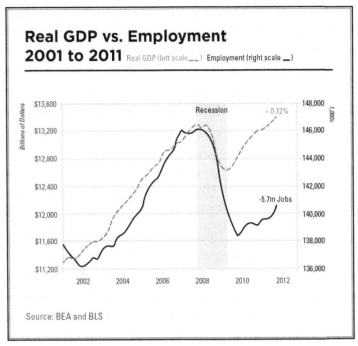

Real GDP vs. Employment
2001 to 2011 Real GDP (left scale ___) Employment (right scale ___)

Source: BEA and BLS

It's led some to speculate that jobless recoveries may be the "new normal." But there is nothing normal about millions of Americans being out of work or toiling away in low-pay positions for which they are overqualified.

Joblessness isn't just a personal tragedy. It's also a national crisis, because it robs our economy of legions of people who want to create and contribute.

As always, our paramount focus must be on strengthening the economy, as increased demand for goods and services is still the strongest driver of job creation. But as the last two economic recoveries have shown, an expanding economy isn't always sufficient to create the jobs we need.

Solving this crisis will require a more creative and flexible response from the U.S. government. Just cutting taxes or increasing spending—which are often the go-to policy options for the right and left—won't cut it.

counting-current-job-recovery-is-slowest-since-truman-was-president/

It's time for policymakers to treat this problem with the urgency it deserves, and to commit to helping create 25 million jobs over the next decade.

There is no time to wait.

PORTRAIT OF THE PROBLEM: UNEMPLOYMENT-PLUS

While GDP growth continues its slow climb back to normalcy, unemployment—which peaked at 10 percent in October 2009—was still above 6 percent in mid-2014, which is high by U.S. historical standards. Five years after the official end of the recession, the job market remains far from healthy.

And the unemployment rate is only part of the story.

Along with the around 9.7 million unemployed Americans,[14] millions more have found themselves working fewer hours than they would like or in jobs far below their skill and education levels. Add in the portion of working-age Americans who have given up looking for work, and you have 12.9 percent of the workforce—some 20 million Americans—either out of work, working fewer hours than they want, or so dejected that they have given up the job hunt altogether.[15][16]

Almost any way you look at it, America's jobs picture is troubling.

- The percentage of Americans in their prime working years—ages 25 to 54—who have jobs is at or near the lowest level in 30 years. The proportion of men who are employed is near a 60-year low.[17]
- Roughly half of all recent college graduates can't find work or are underemployed.[18]
- Roughly 46 million Americans rely on food stamps, an increase of 70 percent since the beginning of 2008.[19]

Particularly alarming is the historically high number of the

---

14 www.bls.gov/news.release/empsit.nr0.htm
15 www.bls.gov/lau/stalt.htm
16 www.dlt.ri.gov/lmi/laus/us/usadj.htm
17 www.bls.gov/data/
18 www.ny.frb.org/research/current_issues/ci20-1.pdf
19 www.frac.org/reports-and-resources/snapfood-stamp-monthly-participation-data/

"long-term unemployed," whose prospects for finding regular full-time jobs decrease with every day they're out of work. About 3.2 million people have been out of work for 27 weeks or more.[20] That's about a third of all unemployed people—double the historical average[21]—and it doesn't include those who've been looking for so long they've given up.

Low-skilled workers are having a particularly tough time in this economy. As of March 2014, according to the Bureau of Labor Statistics, nearly one in ten people with less than a high-school diploma were unemployed.[22]

Also suffering are young people trying to take their first steps into the job market. A 2014 Pew Research Center report found that today's 25- to 32-year-olds are experiencing higher unemployment rates than any generation starting out in the past 50 years.[23] This has consequences that last a lifetime as research shows that young people who graduate from college in a bad economy will be making less money, on average, even decades later when compared to people who entered the job market in a good economy.[24]

Many young people are also vastly underemployed, working fewer hours than they'd like or taking jobs below their skill levels. Almost half of young college graduates are working in jobs that don't require the degrees they earned.[25]

It isn't just the young and unskilled that have a tough time in this job market either, as older workers who lose their jobs tend to stay unemployed longer than others. As of March 2014, the average unemployed person had been out of work for about 36 weeks. For those over 55, the figure was 47 weeks.[26]

20 www.bls.gov/news.release/empsit.nr0.htm
21 www.bostonglobe.com/business/2014/07/05/army-long-term-jobless-dwindles-hiring-quickens/ZAoNj8MKeGLiIHU4pLkF3H/story.html
22 www.bls.gov/news.release/empsit.t04.htm
23 www.pewsocialtrends.org/files/2014/02/SDT-higher-education-FINAL-02-11-2014.pdf
24 www.insights.som.yale.edu/insights/what-has-happened-labor-market-great-recession
25 www.ny.frb.org/research/current_issues/ci20-1.pdf
26 www.aarp.org/content/dam/aarp/research/public_policy_institute/econ_sec/2014/the-employment-situation-march-2014-AARP-ppi-econ-sec.pdf

WHERE ARE THE JOBS?

It's a question that still doesn't have a certain answer.

In this and the following five chapters, we'll look at a number of the factors that are harming job creation, and that must be examined as we develop policy prescriptions for creating 25 million jobs over the next 10 years.

When the Middle Class Isn't Spending, Employers Aren't Hiring

While economists have offered a variety of reasons for the anemic pace of job growth, most agree on one basic premise: A lack of aggregate demand—demand for all goods and services produced by this country—has caused businesses to hire significantly fewer workers than there are people who want to work.

Consumption—household spending on everything from dining out to a visit to the optometrist to purchasing a pair of jeans—accounts for about two-thirds of U.S. economic activity.[27] When the purchasing power of average Americans is on the rise, there is more demand for goods and services, which translates into thriving businesses and increasing numbers of jobs.

In America, consumption often rises or falls with the fortunes of our broad middle class. Unfortunately, the key components of middle-class well-being—namely income and housing values—are not improving sufficiently to spur enough new consumer spending.

Neither real wages (wages adjusted for inflation) nor real total compensation (wages plus benefits adjusted for inflation) has risen during the recovery.[28] As a share of national income, wages and total compensation are at or near their lowest levels since the end of World War II.[29]

Median household income—$51,371, according to the latest U.S. Census figures[30]—remains well below where it was at both the beginning and the end of the Great Recession. Though it has

---

27 www.qz.com/112478/american-consumers-are-being-asked-to-save-the-global-economy-again/
28 www.cbsnews.com/news/stagnant-worker-pay-stunts-us-recovery/
29 www.research.stlouisfed.org/fred2/graph/?g=2Xa
30 www.census.gov/prod/2013pubs/acsbr12-02.pdf

inched up slightly in 2014, median household income has seen a sustained drop during this millennium that is unprecedented in the postwar period.[31] In fact, median household income today is barely higher than it was a quarter century ago, in 1989.[32]

The upshot is that the American middle class—the backbone of our economy in the postwar era—is no longer the most affluent in the world. According to a recent *New York Times* analysis, after-tax middle incomes in Canada are now higher than those in the United States, and lower-income citizens in Europe earn more than their counterparts here. The *Times* noted that "although economic growth in the United States continues to be as strong as in many other countries, or stronger, a small percentage of American households is fully benefiting from it."[33]

The Shrinking Nest Egg

As incomes have dropped or stagnated, so too has the value of many middle-class families' homes. Home ownership has long been the single largest component of wealth for the middle class, the nest egg that many Americans rely on for financial security.

But from 2006 to 2013, U.S. households on net lost roughly $3 trillion in home equity.[34] The housing crash was not typical of most recessions. The four previous economic declines had only minor effects on home equity—in some recessions it even continued to increase.[35]

Though home prices began to rebound in 2013, the value of houses in many hard-hit markets is still well below peak levels of nearly a decade ago.

Studies by the economists Karl Case and Robert Shiller, founders of the home-price indexes that bear their names, show that variations in the housing market—and thus housing wealth—have a significant impact on consumer spending. This

31 www.epi.org/blog/incomes-poverty-stable-wage-stagnation-continues/
32 www.research.stlouisfed.org/fred2/series/MEHOINUSA672N
33 www.nytimes.com/2014/04/23/upshot/the-american-middle-class-is-no-longer-the-worlds-richest.html?ref=business&_r=1
34 www.federalreserve.gov/releases/z1/20100610/accessible/b100.htm
35 www.furmancenter.org/files/publications/HousingandtheGreatRecession.pdf

impact is much greater than, say, changes in stock-market value or financial wealth.

This also has a substantial impact on people's savings, as Americans' median net worth has declined from $88,000 in 2003 to roughly $56,000 in 2013. When adjusted for inflation, that's a staggering 36 percent decrease.[36]

America's poor jobs picture is to some extent a chicken-and-egg problem. The U.S. economy—and job market—is still highly dependent on domestic demand, which depends to a large extent on middle-class spending. But middle-class spending has been stymied by declines in home equity and household income—the latter due in no small measure to job losses and lower wages.

The lack of good jobs hampers consumer demand, which in turn hampers job creation. It's a vicious cycle that must be broken if America is to regain a sound economic footing. If an expanding economy no longer automatically leads to job creation, we know the opposite remains true: more and better jobs will lead to a stronger economy.

The Uncertain Effects of Globalization and Technology

Throughout history, the advent of new technologies—from the wheel to the mechanical reaper to the computer—has changed the nature of work and the lives of workers, sometimes for the worse in the short term, but almost always for the better in the long term.

New inventions have rendered certain kinds of human labor obsolete, but they typically engender increased commerce and productivity so that, after periods of disruption to the existing labor force, they result in the creation of more jobs and greater prosperity.

The recent IT revolution has been no different. Advances in technology, along with freer trade and more open markets, have in general been a boon for societies around the world. Hundreds of millions of people in places like China and India have risen

36 www.nytimes.com/2014/07/27/business/the-typical-household-now-worth-a-third-less.html?emc=eta1

out of poverty and, in turn, become consumers of U.S. goods and services, spurring more job opportunities in America.

But the rising tide of globalization hasn't come without real costs to certain industries and segments of U.S. society.

It is, for example, now cheaper and simpler for companies to manufacture many products and provide certain kinds of services overseas than in the U.S. This has helped keep prices down for American consumers. But it's also cost us a lot of good middle-class jobs. According to the Statistic Brain Research Institute, the U.S. lost 2.6 million jobs to offshore outsourcing in 2013, chiefly in manufacturing, IT services, R&D, distribution, and call/help centers.[37]

For the American workers whose jobs have been lost, it is no comfort to be told that they're victims of "disruptions" in the economy and that they'll eventually see the full benefits of globalization.

They need to be empowered now to find new jobs in new industries that provide real economic opportunity.

The Economic Consequences of Gridlock in Washington

If the jury is still out on the effects of globalization and technology on the American workforce, the verdict is most certainly in on the effects of DC gridlock.

It is harming our economy and making it harder for people to find work.

Washington's inability to solve pressing problems and its recent tendency to govern from crisis to crisis are sowing uncertainty and diminishing confidence throughout our economy.

Most people understand this intuitively. But a team of economists from Stanford and the University of Chicago recently managed to quantify the cost of DC dysfunction. They developed a tool called the Economic Policy Uncertainty Index, which measures the impact of political uncertainty and gridlock on U.S. economic performance.

37 www.statisticbrain.com/outsourcing-statistics-by-country/

Their findings were troubling.

The team found that the increase in policy uncertainty between 2006 and 2011 was associated with a 2.5 percent drop in industrial production and 2.3 million fewer jobs in the United States.[38]

Our government needs to start fueling and stop hurting our economy.

There are numerous ways that government can do it.

Our government can act directly, creating programs that put people to work—for example, by investing in the infrastructure of the country. It can also act indirectly, changing the rules of the road for businesses so employers have more flexibility and more resources to invest, grow, and hire, and workers have more opportunities to be upwardly mobile.

In addition, government can help make sure we have a workforce prepared to meet the challenges of today's job market.

In the following five chapters we'll examine a wide range of options and approaches—some reforms of existing policies, some ideas for entirely new programs, innovations, and partnerships—that could reinvigorate the economy.

It will take rethinking our current approach to a number of specific policy areas including taxation and regulations, investments in infrastructure and R&D, immigration, education and health care. But no goal is more important to the American people than jobs—not just any jobs, but good jobs that sustain families—for the twenty-first century.

Tax and Regulatory Reform To Spur Investment in Infrastructure

Over the years, one area of broad bipartisan agreement has been the value of government investment in infrastructure and research. These investments in highways, dams, bridges, and power grids, as well as medical and scientific research, have

---

38 www.economics.uchicago.edu/workshops/Baker%20Scott%20%20
    Measuring%20Economics%20Policy%20Uncertainty.pdf

provided critical building blocks for our economy—and thus, scores and scores of valuable, dependable jobs.

Many commercial innovations—from the Internet to GPS to memory-foam mattresses—got their start in government or government-funded research labs.

But these critical federal investments have declined precipitously in recent decades.

As noted by William Galston of the Brookings Institution, total U.S. public spending on infrastructure "has fallen steadily since the 1960s and is now at around 2.4 percent of GDP. Europe, on the other hand, invests 5 percent of GDP in its infrastructure, and China invests 9 percent."[39]

Failure to maintain, renovate, and expand our infrastructure has had serious consequences for our national well-being and competitiveness. Instead of leading the world in transportation, shipping, and power facilities, the U.S. ranks "18th in railroads, 19th in ports, 20th in roads, 30th in airports, and 33rd in the quality of our electrical system," writes Galston, citing the World Economic Forum's 2012-2013 Global Competitiveness Report.[40]

The American economy pays a steep price for our lack of investment in infrastructure. The American Society of Civil Engineers reports that by 2020, if the mounting investment gap in the nation's infrastructure is not addressed, "the economy is expected to lose almost $1 trillion in business sales, resulting in a loss of 3.5 million jobs," and "the cumulative cost to the economy will be more than $3.1 trillion in GDP and $1.1 trillion in total trade."[41]

This projected decline in jobs would affect all skill levels within construction, engineering, and other fields.

Government investment in research and development has plummeted as well. Federally funded research of the kind that helped jump-start many breakthroughs in information

---

39 www.pwfinance.net/document/research_reports/Brookings%20NIB.pdf
40 www.brookings.edu/blogs/up-front/posts/2013/01/23-crumbling-infrastructure-galston
41 www.asce.org/uploadedfiles/Infrastructure/failure_to_act/failure_to_act_report.pdf

technology, for example, has declined from 1.3 percent of GDP in the 1960s to 0.8 percent today, according to the National Research Council.[42]

But just saying that the government needs to spend more money on the nation's infrastructure and R&D isn't going to cut it in these fiscally constrained times. We need to find creative ways to finance new projects and provide incentives for private-sector investment.

One way to stimulate further investments in infrastructure, research and other economy-enhancing priorities is to reform our tax and regulatory system in a way that gives businesses more flexibility, freeing up more resources for job creation and growth.

What follows are ideas for reforms of our tax code—some directly linked to infrastructure investments—as well as ideas for a more streamlined approach to regulation that can spur more investment of all kinds.

IDEAS: MAKING OUR TAX CODE SIMPLER, FAIRER, AND MORE ENCOURAGING TO JOB CREATION

Both Democrats and Republicans favor tax reform that would make our tax code simpler, fairer, and more conducive to job creation and wage growth. It sounds great in theory, but the details are a lot tougher. That's why Washington hasn't delivered comprehensive tax reform since 1986, when Republican President Ronald Reagan and Democratic House Speaker Tip O'Neill came together to get it done.

Since then, our tax code has only become more complex and more inefficient. Still, tax reform efforts stall again and again. The latest was the bipartisan effort from Representative Dave Camp, the Republican chairman of the House Committee on Ways and Means, who sought to lower rates and pay for them by eliminating a number of deductions and credits. But even before the plan was released in early 2014, it was dismissed by

---

42 www.appropriations.senate.gov/sites/default/files/hearings/
   Massachusetts%20Institute%20of%20Technology%20-%20OWT.pdf

both parties as "dead on arrival" because it contained too many controversial measures in an election year and deal-breakers for each party.

"Every press release was the same: 'Chairman Camp should be admired for being a great guy and doing a great thing, BUT...,'" says tax expert Martin A. Sullivan, chief economist for Tax Analysts.

Sullivan says that given current political realities, we may need to look beyond conventional tax measures if we're ever going to see serious reform.

"You have two types of tax reform," he says. "You have your 1986, Reagan-style broaden-the-base, lower-the-rate tax reform, which is a very good thing to do. And that's what Camp does. And then you have outside-the-box tax reform. Because we seem to have hit a dead end with conventional tax reform, maybe there will be a market for more radical ideas."

Before we explore some of those "outside-the-box" ideas, let's take a look at the Camp bill. Though it did not pass this time around, it did feature a number of components that have been supported by both Democrats and Republicans.

Here are some key features of Camp's Tax Reform Act of 2014:[43]

- Lower rates for individuals and businesses: On the corporate side, the plan would reduce the top rate from 35 percent to 25 percent. On the individual side, instead of the current seven individual income rates that range from 10 to 39.6 percent, there would be three: 10, 25, and 35 percent, with the highest bracket applying to the income that today is subject to the 39.6 percent bracket ($400,000 for singles and $450,000 for married couples filing jointly).
- Larger standard deduction: The plan would raise the standard deduction to $11,000 for individuals and $22,000 for married couples to incentivize fewer taxpayers to itemize their deductions.

43 www.money.cnn.com/2014/02/26/pf/taxes/house-republican-tax-reform-dave-camp/

- Larger child tax credit: Increased from $1,000 to $1,500 per child and available for kids up to the age of 18 instead of 17. Also eventually phases out the child tax credit for very high-income filers.
- Reduced mortgage-interest deduction: The mortgage-interest deduction currently allowed on mortgages up to $1 million would be lowered to a cap of $500,000.
- Change in the way capital gains are taxed: Long-term capital gains and dividends would be taxed as ordinary income, but 40 percent of the gains would be exempt from taxation.
- Corporate and individual alternative minimum tax (AMT) repealed.
- Permanent R&D incentive: Reforms and makes permanent a research-and-development tax credit.
- Investments in infrastructure: Dedicates $126.5 billion to the Highway Trust Fund (see more explanation below) through a tax break on foreign profits.
- New bank tax: Large financial institutions would pay a quarterly tax on assets in excess of $500 billion, a provision intended to raise more than $86 billion over 10 years.

For more details about the Camp bill, go to:
www.waysandmeans.house.gov/news/documentsingle.
aspx?DocumentID=370987

Beyond the Camp bill are several other, less conventional ideas that have gained some traction among members of both parties:

Replace or Reduce Personal Income Tax for Most Americans with a Value Added Tax (VAT)

There are several plans for consumption taxes that have piqued interest on both sides over the last several years and that are considered simpler and distributionally neutral—meaning they wouldn't shift the burden from taxpayers in one income bracket to those in another or create winners and losers within income classes.

- "The Competitive Tax Plan," proposed by Columbia University tax law professor and former Treasury official Michael J. Graetz, is a broad-based tax on goods and services—modeled after VATs in Canada, Australia, and Singapore. At 12.9 percent, Graetz says it would produce enough revenue to exempt families earning under $100,000—the vast majority of U.S. households—from paying any personal income tax. Households earning above that amount would pay a reduced tax rate. And the corporate income tax would be lowered to 15 percent. The plan aims to shield low- and moderate-income workers from an increased tax burden through payroll tax cuts and expanded refundable tax credits for children, delivered through debit cards that can be used at the cash register. See more details about this plan at: *www.law.columbia.edu/null/download?&exclusive=filemgr.download&file_id=622913*

- "The X Tax," first proposed by the late Princeton economist David Bradford and later adapted by American Enterprise Institute's Alan Viard and Ernst and Young's Robert Carroll, is a progressive VAT. Under this plan, according to Viard, households are taxed on their wages under a progressive rate schedule, with higher tax rates on higher-paid workers and exemptions and tax credits for low-paid workers. Households are not taxed on income from savings. Businesses are taxed on their cash flow at a flat rate equal to the rate on the highest-paid workers. Firms are allowed to immediately deduct all of their investment costs rather than depreciating them over a period of years. For more details, see: *www.aei.org/outlook/economics/fiscal-policy/the-x-tax-the-progressive-consumption-tax-america-needs/*

Reform the Way Corporations' Overseas Profits Are Taxed

Under the current U.S. tax system, multinational companies are required to pay taxes on earnings made abroad when they are brought back to the United States, even if those earnings were already taxed in the foreign countries. Many businesses would like to see the U.S. adopt elements of the territorial tax system that many other industrialized countries have, where profits are taxed only in the country where they are earned. Proponents of this reform believe it would encourage U.S. companies to bring home some of the roughly $2 trillion in corporate profits currently being held offshore and invest in the U.S.[44]

A number of ideas have been proposed to reform the taxation of overseas profits in ways that encourage more investment in America.

- "The Partnership To Build America Act," introduced by Representative John Delaney (D-MD), would allow multinational companies to bring their overseas profits home tax-free if they agree to invest a portion of those profits in a fund—the American Infrastructure Fund—to finance the rebuilding of our country's transportation, energy, communications, water, and education infrastructure. Representative Delaney says that this financing vehicle, launched with $50 billion in capital entirely from the private sector, could amount to a $750 billion revolving fund. As of summer 2014, the bill, and a companion bill in the Senate, had the backing of 46 Republicans, 41 Democrats, and 1 independent.[45][46] For more details on this plan, see: *www.delaney.house.gov/infrastructure/ information-on-congressman-delaneys-infrastructure-bill*

- Expanded International Cooperation, proposed in a 2014 paper by Eric Toder, co-director of the Urban-Brookings Tax Policy Center, and Alan

---

44 www.bloomberg.com/news/2014-03-12/cash-abroad-rises-206-billion-as-apple-to-ibm-avoid-tax.html
45 www.govtrack.us/congress/bills/113/hr2084
46 www.govtrack.us/congress/bills/113/s1957

Viard, resident scholar at the American Enterprise Institute, would call on the countries that are home to most of the large multinational corporations to agree on how to divide global corporate tax revenues. Such an approach, the authors say, would not only prevent the shifting of income to tax havens but also allow countries a large degree of control over corporate tax policy. The U.S. would eliminate its taxation of foreign profits brought back home. For more information on this idea, see: *www.aei.org/ files/2014/04/03/-toder-viard-report_132524981261.pdf*

- A provision in Representative Camp's tax-reform plan would allow U.S. corporations to bring profits earned by foreign subsidiaries in previous years back to this country at a substantially lower tax rate—8.75 percent for cash or cash equivalents and 3.5 percent for earnings that have been reinvested in the subsidiary's property, plant, or equipment.[47] These taxes would be payable over eight years.[48] The revenues from this one-time tax on accumulated profits would be deposited into the federal Highway Trust Fund to address the funding shortfall that currently exists for federal transportation infrastructure projects. Representative Camp says the proposal would raise $126.5 billion for the Highway Trust Fund, enough to eliminate the cumulative shortfall and keep the trust fund solvent through 2021.[49]

IDEAS: STRIKING THE RIGHT BALANCE WITH REGULATORY REFORM

Leaders in both parties have noted the need to streamline America's complex regulatory system. There are, of course,

47 www.forbes.com/sites/taxanalysts/2014/03/03/twenty-five-interesting-features-of-chairman-camps-new-tax-reform-plan/2/

48 www.taxvox.taxpolicycenter.org/2014/02/27/how-does-dave-camp-pay-for-individual-tax-cuts-by-raising-revenue-from-corporations/

49 www.politico.com/morningtransportation/0214/morningtransportation13137.html

fundamental disagreements between Democrats and Republicans about when and where it is appropriate for government to regulate.

But one area of common ground to start from may be addressing what economists at the Progressive Policy Institute (PPI) refer to as "regulatory accumulation," the natural buildup of regulations over time that has resulted "in a maze of duplicative and outdated rules companies must comply with."[50]

They propose the creation of an independent Regulatory Improvement Commission that would review existing regulations and send a package of recommended changes to Congress. Here's a look at the PPI proposal as well as two other ideas that relate specifically to new businesses.

Regulatory Improvement Commission

As proposed by Michael Mandel and Diana G. Carew of the Progressive Policy Institute, a new federal Regulatory Improvement Commission (RIC) would objectively examine the cumulative impact of a selected portion of the regulatory code and submit a package of recommended improvements to Congress for an up-or-down vote. The RIC would be modeled on the Base Closure and Realignment Commission (BRAC) that reviewed the status of military installations.[51]

Cost-benefit Analysis

Direct the CBO and OMB to conduct a third-party analysis of economic costs and benefits of all proposed regulations, including their impact in relation to existing federal, state, and local regulations, focusing especially on their effects on new and small businesses.[52]

---

50 www.progressivepolicy.org/issues/economy/regulatory-improvement-commission-a-politically-viable-approach-to-u-s-regulatory-reform/
51 Michael Mandel and Diana G. Carew, Progressive Policy Institute, *"Regulatory Improvement Commission: A Politically-Viable Approach to U.S. Regulatory Reform,"* May 2013.
52 Dearie, J., & Geduldig, C. (2013). *Where the Jobs Are: Entrepreneurship and the Soul of the American Economy.* Wiley.

50-State Ranking

Have the Commerce Department, in partnership with entrepreneurship organizations around the country, develop a research framework by which to rank all 50 states according to their regulatory friendliness to new business formation and growth.[53]

IDEAS: PROMOTE INVESTMENT IN AMERICA'S INFRASTRUCTURE AND BASIC R&D

In more prosperous times, America's infrastructure—its highways, bridges, dams, power grids, and more—was the envy of the world. Today, much of America's infrastructure is crumbling. And there's a simple reason: Public investment in our nation's infrastructure as a percentage of GDP is half what it was 50 years ago.[54]

Investment in infrastructure has played a crucial role in America's economic development—as Galston notes, "from the canals and roadways of the early 19th century to the Civil War-era Transcontinental Railroad … to FDR's bridges, tunnels, and airports that put millions back to work during the Great Depression, to Dwight Eisenhower's visionary Interstate Highway System, begun in the 1950s and still benefitting the nation two generations later."[55]

As history has shown, smart infrastructure investments lead to job growth. Even with the significant decline in U.S. infrastructure investment relative to GDP, infrastructure jobs still accounted for 11 percent of national employment in 2012.[56]

And infrastructure occupations tend to offer better wages compared to all occupations nationally.[57]

There is little question, then, why policymakers of all stripes have urged greater investment in U.S. infrastructure.

53 Dearie, J., & Geduldig, C. (2013). *Where the Jobs Are: Entrepreneurship and the Soul of the American Economy.* Wiley.
54 www.cfr.org/infrastructure/encouraging-us-infrastructure-investment/p27771
55 www.brookings.edu/blogs/up-front/posts/2013/01/23-crumbling-infrastructure-galston
56 www.brookings.edu/research/interactives/2014/infrastructure-jobs#/M10420
57 www.brookings.edu/research/interactives/2014/infrastructure-jobs#/M10420

Two ideas, by Representatives John Delaney (D-MD) and Dave Camp (R-MI), for helping finance infrastructure improvements through repatriated overseas corporate profits are discussed in the section above on tax reform. But there have also been calls from both business and labor, Democrats and Republicans, for a broader, more permanent fix. Similar calls have been made for restoring funding for basic research of the kind that spurred the medical, communications, and other technological breakthroughs of previous decades, and for incentivizing private-sector research.

Create a National Infrastructure Bank

Many of America's economic competitors have some kind of national infrastructure bank, which relies on relatively small government investments to attract significantly larger multiples of other public and private-sector investment.

Under most current proposals, a U.S. National Infrastructure Bank would be established as an independent, government-owned corporation with bipartisan leadership.

The bank would be funded initially with federal appropriations ranging, under various proposals, from $5 billion for each of its first five years[58] to as much as $60 billion to leverage funding by other public and private investor-depositors in a wide range of infrastructure projects.[59] After an initial period of federal funding, the bank—with a permanent professional staff to provide financial and technical advice—would become financially independent.

In addition to transportation, the bank would be eligible to invest in a wide array of infrastructure projects, including technology, environmental and energy projects, public utilities, and the renovation of schools and hospitals.[60]

---

58 www.delauro.house.gov/index.php?option=com_content&view
   =article&id=572:infrastructure-bank-legislation-garners-strong-
   support&catid=9&Itemid=25

59 www.politifact.com/truth-o-meter/promises/obameter/promise/31/
   create-a-60-billion-bank-to-fund-roads-and-bridge/

60 www.brookings.edu/research/papers/2012/12/13-infrastructure-bank-
   galston-davis

Accelerate Innovation

- R&D tax credit: Restore the research-and-development tax credit by raising the alternative simplified R&D credit from the current 14 percent to at least 20 percent (or 45 percent to regain its previous level) and make it permanent.[61]

- Increase funding of basic research: To spur greater applied research and development by the private sector, restore federal funding of basic research from its current level below 1 percent of GDP to 2 percent of GDP annually.

Immigration Reform

We can't look at the U.S. workforce, either high-skilled, low-skilled or everything in between, without considering an issue of utmost importance to employers and workers alike: the impact of U.S. immigration policies on the job picture and the economy in general.

Immigrants have always played an essential role in the U.S. economy. In fact, immigrants are responsible for launching about half of the country's most successful start-ups as well as many of our most valuable patents.[62]

Despite this fact, the United States continues to make it difficult for talented immigrants to come and to stay here.

Of course, America's immigration system is a complicated affair, and one that affects much more than just the employment picture. As millions of immigrants, some legal, some not, make their homes here, there are implications for the entire U.S. economy, for local communities with sizable immigrant populations, and certain groups of residents who might find themselves in competition for jobs. There are also legal considerations, as scores of foreign nationals have crossed our borders, or tried to, without going through the proper

61 www2.itif.org/2012-fifty-ways-competitiveness-woes-behind.pdf
62 www.economist.com/news/business/21587778-americas-engines-growth-are-misfiring-badly-not-open-business

legal channels.

In the summer of 2014, we got a vivid reminder of the many emotionally fraught dimensions of the immigration issue as tens of thousands of undocumented immigrants from Central America,[63] many of them children and many of them fleeing gangs and violence back home, poured into the country across the U.S.–Mexico border.

There were no easy answers then. There are still no easy answers. But, as we engage in this complex and heated debate on immigration—and we have to—there are reform ideas that enjoy broad bipartisan support and could provide much-needed benefits and enrichment to both the economy and fabric of this country.

For starters, many employers say that it's difficult to find candidates with high-quality science, technology, engineering, and mathematics—or STEM—backgrounds. And we know that a good portion of U.S. college graduates in STEM fields are international students. International students accounted for 57 percent of full-time enrollment in U.S. graduate engineering programs in fall 2012, according to *US News*.[64]

But many of those students are not eligible to stay in America to use the education they've received here.

Under current immigration laws, a maximum of 85,000 high-skilled foreign workers[65] can be hired under the H-1B visa program to work temporarily in the U.S. in jobs where workers are in short supply. This year, as in most, the cap was reached less than a week after applications were accepted.[66]

The tech industry is among those pushing for major immigration reform that would allow more U.S.-educated engineers, scientists, computer programmers, and others to become a part of the workforce. Last year, for instance, Facebook CEO Mark Zuckerberg launched a political action

---

63 www.ctmirror.org/latino-advocates-knock-malloy-on-central-american-immigrant-children-decision/
64 www.news.yahoo.com/engineering-schools-most-international-students-150517906.html
65 www.cnbc.com/id/101456282
66 www.bipartisanpolicy.org/blog/immigration/2014/04/01/h-1b-visa-cap-expected-be-hit-within-days

group called FWD.us to push for such reform.

Of course, immigrants' importance to our economy isn't just in high-tech and high-value start-ups. Immigrants play an essential role in agriculture, construction, and other critical sectors of our economy.

What's more, effective immigration reform could even help solve some of our budget and social safety net challenges. Both Medicare and Social Security are being strained by the same inexorable demographic trend of fewer workers being available to pay for current benefits.

An immigration solution that secured our borders and provided more essential workers and entrepreneurs for our economy would also provide more of the tax revenue necessary to shore up programs like Medicare and Social Security.

We've watched over the past several months how the flaws in America's immigration system have reached a crisis point. We know the system is broken—that there are, on the one hand, too many people coming here and living here illegally at the same time that it's becoming tougher for talented immigrants to work, invent, and innovate in America.

It's time we find responsible, commonsense solutions.

IDEAS: WIN-WIN IMMIGRATION REFORMS

Despite the heated rhetoric in the immigration debate, there is actually broad bipartisan consensus on the urgency of immigration reform and the outlines of a possible solution.

In June 2013, a sweeping bipartisan bill to overhaul our immigration policies passed the Senate, with 14 Republicans crossing the aisle to join Democrats in support of the bill. The bill would have offered a path to citizenship for millions of undocumented residents by creating new visas for foreign workers in low-skill jobs, devoting billions of dollars to bolstering security on the U.S. southern border, and allowing more foreign students to stay here to work at high-skill jobs after receiving their educations.[67] But the bill couldn't make it out of

67 www.immigrationpolicy.org/special-reports/guide-s744-understanding-

the House of Representatives.

The Senate immigration bill wasn't enacted, and many critics wonder whether a comprehensive bill is the best way to go, compared to a step-by-step approach. Still, it offers a good starting point for discussions of a potential deal. Here are the key points of the Senate bill that relate to the labor market,[68] along with several other ideas that could have a major impact on job growth in the years ahead.

A Path to Citizenship

- Registered provisional immigrant status: The roughly 11 million people living in the U.S. illegally could obtain "registered provisional immigrant status" in six months' time if they meet certain requirements. Ten years after that, they could seek a green card and lawful permanent-resident status if they've paid taxes, learned English, and met work and other requirements.

- Quicker road for children: Those brought here as children would be eligible for green cards in five years and citizenship immediately after.

- Enhanced border security requirement: Permanent-resident status for undocumented immigrants would be dependent on certain border-security requirements being met within 10 years, including the doubling of the number of agents along the U.S.–Mexico border, new pedestrian fencing, new surveillance towers, and other technologies. This $46.3 billion investment in border enforcement would aim for 100 percent surveillance of the border and 90 percent effectiveness (meaning 9 out of 10 who attempt to cross the border without permission would be apprehended).

2013-senate-immigration-bill
68 Associated Press, "Details of the Senate immigration bill," June 12, 2013

Increase Number of High-skilled Workers

- Expand H-1B visa program: The cap on the H-1B program, which allows U.S. employers to temporarily employ foreign workers in high-skilled or specialty fields, would be increased from 85,000 to 110,000 a year, with an additional 25,000 for those with an advanced degree in a STEM field from a U.S. school. The cap could be expanded depending on demand.

- Exempt certain professionals from green-card limits: Immigrants with extraordinary skills, such as executives of multinationals, athletes, physicians in specialty fields, professors, researchers, and graduates of U.S. universities with advanced degrees in STEM fields would be exempt from green-card caps.

- Merit-based visas: A new merit visa for up to 250,000 people a year would award points to prospective immigrants based on a number of attributes such as education, employment, and length of stay in this country. Those with the most points would receive these visas.

- Start-up visas: A "start-up visa" would be available to foreign entrepreneurs who want to start a company in the U.S.

- Repeal of diversity visas: To offset the additional merit- and employment-related visas, the government's Diversity Visa Lottery Program, which awards 55,000 visas to people from countries with historically low rates of immigration, would be eliminated.

Increase Number of Lower-skilled Workers

- Guest worker "W-visas:" A new "W-visa" would allow up to 200,000 low-skilled workers per year to come to the U.S. for jobs in fields such as construction, long-term care, and hospitality.

- Path to legal status for agricultural workers: Farm

workers already here illegally who've worked in the industry for two years could qualify for green-card status in another five years if they continue to work in agriculture.

For more details about the Senate bill, go to: *www.gpo.gov/ fdsys/pkg/CRPT-113srpt40/pdf/CRPT-113srpt40.pdf*

Beyond the Senate Bill

While the Senate bill encompasses a broad range of ideas, other ideas proposed recently have merited some bipartisan support:

- Eliminating the H-1B caps: A number of business executives, especially in tech fields, have argued for eliminating the cap on H-1B visas altogether or greatly relaxing the current restrictions. Speaking on a technology panel in 2005, Microsoft Chairman Bill Gates said visa restrictions were keeping too many bright, educated people from working here. "A policy that limits too many smart people coming to the United States is questionable," he said. "The visa issue doesn't make sense."[69]

- Awarding "graduation" green cards: Some immigration experts have proposed awarding a permanent residency card, or green card, to any foreign-born student meeting national security requirements who graduates from a U.S. university with an undergraduate or advanced degree in a STEM field.

Education and Training: Preparing the Workforce For the Jobs of Today and Tomorrow

Jeffrey Immelt, CEO of GE, noted some years ago that more students in the United States were graduating with degrees in

69 David A Vise, "Gates Cites Hiring Woes, Criticizes Visa Restrictions," Washington Post, April 28, 2005.

sports exercise than in electrical engineering. "So if we want to be the massage capital of the world," he famously quipped, "we're well on our way."

Report after report in the last decade has echoed Immelt's sentiments, sounding alarm bells about the country's decline in math and science education and thus our ability to prosper in an increasingly competitive global economy.

Many companies complain that schools and colleges are not providing adequate basic education to students who will enter the workforce in the fields that are flourishing in the twenty-first century. They often talk of a "skills gap," or mismatch between the skills they need and the skills their job applicants possess.

Though there is still debate about the extent of such a "skills gap," the latest employment numbers suggest a real problem. The Bureau of Labor Statistics reports that, although there are roughly 10 million unemployed,[70] there are about 4.5 million open jobs[71]—jobs that employers say they want to fill but can't find qualified applicants for. Something is clearly wrong with that equation.

The same picture emerges when you look at the issue through the lens of specific industries. Retired Lockheed Martin Chairman Norman Augustine, for instance, has cited a critical shortfall of engineers in the U.S.

And Microsoft published a report in 2012 warning that there would not be enough college graduates with degrees in computer science to fill the over 120,000 projected U.S. job openings each year in computing occupations.[72]

A 2012 report by the President's Council of Advisors on Science and Technology concluded that one million more STEM professionals would be needed in the U.S. workforce in the next decade—above and beyond those already on track to graduate—if the United States wants to remain economically competitive.[73]

Some economists and academics take issue with the concept

---

70 www.bls.gov/news.release/empsit.t01.htm#cps_empsit_a01.f.1
71 www.bls.gov/news.release/pdf/jolts.pdf
72 www.microsoft.com/en-us/news/download/presskits/citizenship/msnts. pdf
73 www.whitehouse.gov/sites/default/files/microsites/ostp/pcast-engage-to-excel-final_2-25-12.pdf

of a skills gap, arguing that if such a gap really existed, it would manifest itself in increased wages. Peter Cappelli, a professor at the Wharton School of Business, examined hiring complaints and found other factors at work, including employers unwilling to provide in-house job training.

"A generation ago, employers would hire and train employees," says Cappelli, author of *Why Good People Can't Get Jobs: The Skills Gap and What Companies Can Do About It.* "Now they demand trained workers. They want experienced candidates who can contribute immediately with no training or start-up time."[74]

Whatever the extent of the skills gap, few question the need for a workforce that's better prepared to meet the needs and challenges of the twenty-first-century global economy. That means more and better STEM education, more measures directing students to the critical high-tech and information-age fields of the future, and ultimately, a more technologically sophisticated workforce that cannot only fill jobs that exist, but lead the way to greater productivity, innovation, and entrepreneurship.

IDEAS: MORE PARTNERSHIPS AND STEM INCENTIVES

President Obama has embraced the goal of one million more STEM graduates in the next decade. But, as the Business-Higher Education Forum (BHEF), an organization of Fortune 500 CEOs and prominent college presidents, notes, "[The creation of one million new STEM graduates] will require a large-scale disruption of the undergraduate education practices."[75]

In other words, it won't just happen on its own. It's going to require bold moves.

This is a complex problem that won't be solved by just encouraging more high-school kids to study biology. In a 2013 report on "STEM Attrition," the National Center for Education Statistics found that of students entering STEM fields, 48 percent

74 www.business.time.com/2012/06/04/the-skills-gap-myth-why-companies-cant-find-good-people/
75 www.bhef.com/sites/g/files/g829556/f/201306/report_2013_stem_undergrad_model.pdf

of bachelor's degree students and 69 percent of associate's degree students didn't complete their studies. Roughly one-half switched to non-STEM fields, and the rest left college before earning a degree or certificate.[76]

So along with efforts to recruit and direct students to STEM fields, we need to find ways to keep them there or at least match those students who do leave with jobs that may require some math or tech skills if not a degree.

All over the country, elected officials at the state and local levels, business leaders, and academics are responding to the challenge and coming up with innovative programs and partnerships.

Some examples: Ohio State has teamed with IBM to address the need for a workforce with stronger analytical skills.[77] The University of Maryland, College Park, is partnering with Northrup Grumman to create the nation's first residential undergraduate cybersecurity honors program.[78] The University of Wisconsin system is working with the Milwaukee Water Council and other regional stakeholders to graduate trained professionals in the water industry with the hope that they can come up with much-needed new approaches to sustainability issues.[79]

With so much at stake—good jobs, as well as our nation's status as a global leader in innovation—the federal government needs to support the programs already underway and encourage the development of more partnerships and better alignment of education with workforce needs.

Though it's worth examining how our education system is preparing students for the realities of the twenty-first-century job market from the kindergarten level on up, the best leverage point for the government in the face of the current shortage of STEM professionals is at the undergraduate education level, whether through community colleges or four-year institutions.

76 www.nces.ed.gov/pubs2014/2014001rev.pdf
77 www.ohiohighered.org/sites/ohiohighered.org/files/uploads/board/ condition-report/2014-Conditions-Report_FINAL.pdf
78 www.bhef.com/our-work/regional-projects/umd-system-northrop-grumman
79 BHEF/ACT Policy Brief, "Building the Talent Pipeline: Policy Recommendations for The Condition of STEM 2013," April 2014.

Here are several actions that people involved in workforce training and education recommend that the federal government consider:

Fund the Redesign of Introductory-level College Courses across All STEM Majors

The BHEF in partnership with ACT, a nonprofit organization best known for its college-admissions testing, recommends that federal agencies overseeing STEM education, particularly the National Science Foundation, provide incentives to colleges and universities to redesign introductory courses across all STEM majors.

According to a recent BHEF/ACT policy report, these freshman- and sophomore-level classes could, with the help of business, provide hands-on research experiences and mentoring and internship opportunities for students, expose them to emerging fields such as data science and cybersecurity, and explain how these emerging fields could fit into a course of study. The report suggests that if students had this type of knowledge and experience at the beginning of their undergraduate education, they'd be more likely to complete their degree within a STEM field and more likely to gravitate to areas where jobs are currently available or where growth is expected.[80]

Tax Deduction for STEM Graduates

In conversations with business leaders and entrepreneurs across the country, John Dearie and Courtney Geduldig—authors of the book *Where the Jobs Are*—heard frequent complaints that the U.S. education system wasn't producing graduates with the skills and training twenty-first-century companies needed. Among the authors' ideas was a $50,000 federal tax deduction for any student who completes an undergraduate or postgraduate degree in a STEM field. Graduates could deduct up to $10,000 per year from their taxable income over the initial five years of postgraduate employment.

80 www.bhef.com/sites/g/files/g829556/f/201406/2014_brief_BHEF_ACT_0.pdf

Bring Business and Education Together

Dearie and Geduldig recommend that the government launch a national dialogue between business groups and education leaders to examine all levels of curricula to ensure our education system is best serving the needs of students as well as twenty-first-century businesses. One particular focus, they note, could be the nation's roughly 1,200 community colleges,[81] which they say are a keystone of the nation's workforce-development efforts.

The authors note that in Europe, community college and vocational educations are a vital asset that dovetails with the needs of the labor market. Most high-school graduates throughout northern and central Europe, they say, choose vocational-education programs that combine classroom and workplace learning for several years and result in a certificate or credential that has significant value in the labor market.

Fund STEM-related Courses for Non-STEM Majors

With increasing numbers of jobs using various levels of STEM skill—an increase of nearly 60 percent since 1980, according to the Georgetown University Center on Education and the Workforce[82]—the government could provide grants to higher-education institutions to develop new courses for non-STEM majors. These courses would introduce students to the kinds of analytical and quantitative skills that employers say they're looking for, according to the BHEF/ACT report.

Continue to fund basic research

With the federal government responsible for the majority of basic research in the U.S.,[83] any retrenchment on funding—such as the reductions that initially resulted from "sequestration"—contributes to an innovation deficit with real consequences for the development of new technologies as well as the labor market.

Much basic research and development in this country takes

---

81 www.aacc.nche.edu/ABOUTCC/Pages/default.aspx
82 www.georgetown.app.box.com/s/tlfsn8vah39oyb42tpyi
83 www.washingtonpost.com/blogs/wonkblog/wp/2013/02/26/the-coming-rd-crash/

place at universities, with corporations and businesses tapping into that research to commercialize new technologies and innovations. These university labs are also the training ground for graduate students. When funding is not guaranteed, as was the case when the sequester cuts put projects on hold and eliminated positions at university labs throughout the country, there were news reports of students suggesting that they may rethink their career paths.

A broad coalition of business and higher-education leaders, as well as many Democrats and Republicans in DC, are generally united on the importance of continued and even expanded funding of basic research at the federal level.

Stoking America's Entrepreneurial Fire

Everyone likes a good creation story. That moment where it all began. And in America, we love one in particular.

The story of the great entrepreneur.

You know the one: The genius toiling away in the garage with nothing but an idea, a pocket protector, and a relentless desire to succeed.

At least, that is how the story goes. And there are many like it, featuring characters with names like Ford, Jobs, Gates, and Zuckerberg.

These stories aren't false. These entrepreneurs were and are exceptional innovators.

But the stories also contain an essential fiction—a myth—that has serious implications for our economy.

The myth is that great ideas and great companies are born almost entirely of individual greatness.

But real-life entrepreneurship is a lot more complicated.

Entrepreneurs may be born, but they can only grow if they are in the right ecosystem.

And unfortunately, that ecosystem has broken down in many parts of America.

Why should we care?

Because entrepreneurship is essential to creating the 25 million jobs America needs over the next decade.

America's entrepreneurial culture is one of the main reasons that our economy has led the world for the last century. In fact, research by the Kauffman Foundation and others has shown that the bulk of new job creation in the U.S. in recent decades has been the result of new business formation.[84][85]

So it should concern us that the number of start-ups created in the U.S. is still well off pre-recession highs in 2006.[86][87] Not only are there fewer start-ups, but new businesses are also hiring fewer workers than they have historically.

Why is this happening?

In their recently released book, *Where the Jobs Are*, authors John Dearie and Courtney Geduldig try to provide an answer. For the book, they held roundtable discussions with entrepreneurs across the country to learn why fewer new businesses are being launched. There was surprising consensus, with many entrepreneurs citing:

- Lack of access to capital in the wake of the financial crisis and the loss of home equity due to the housing-market collapse;
- A dramatic decline in the number—and investment activity—of venture-capital funds;
- Costly new regulatory hurdles and other obstacles to taking small companies public;
- Regulatory overload and the high costs of compliance in general; and
- A tax structure that can disrupt cash flow needed for reinvestment in small, growing businesses.

These problems must be addressed. If we don't find ways to encourage more entrepreneurial activity, the hopes and dreams of America's workers will go unfulfilled.

---

84 www.kauffman.org/what-we-do/research/firm-formation-and-growth-series/the-importance-of-startups-in-job-creation-and-job-destruction
85 www.nber.org/papers/w16300
86 www.bls.gov/bdm/entrepreneurship/entrepreneurship.htm
87 www.aei-ideas.org/2014/05/declining-us-business-dynamism-its-for-real-and-its-spectacular-i-mean-spectacularly-worrisome/

IDEAS: GIVING START-UPS A LEG UP

As Dearie and Geduldig point out in their book, new businesses have for decades been the chief source of new job creation in America. But according to an August 2014 study by the Brookings Institution, entrepreneurship and the rate of new business creation is on the decline in the U.S.[88]

As a result of their talks with entrepreneurs, Dearie and Geduldig outlined a number of targeted government incentives that could facilitate the founding of new businesses and spur the creation of more jobs.

It's important to note that these targeted incentives often work against the goals of more comprehensive tax reform efforts (such as the Rep. Camp proposal), which typically seeks to simplify and broaden the tax base. But considering the difficulty of passing comprehensive tax reform, we have included these ideas—and other incentives like them—for your consideration.

Establish a new "E-Corp"

Have the Internal Revenue Service establish a new entrepreneur, or "E-Corp," tax status under which new businesses would be subject to a flat 5 percent income tax for the first five years, allowing them to reinvest most of what they earn, preserve cash flow, and eliminate tax complexity and uncertainty.

Enhance entrepreneurs' access to capital

- Favorable accounting: Allow new businesses to use the cash method of accounting during their first five years of operation. Permit 100 percent first-year expensing of business-related capital, equipment, off-the-shelf software, and real-estate investment costs for the first five years. Allow new businesses with no taxable earnings in certain years during their initial five years of operation to carry forward the deduction of such expenses for 15 years beyond the year in

---

88 www.vox.com/2014/8/5/5968783/entrepreneurial-decline-litan

which they were incurred. Also for the first five years, allow new firms to deduct research-and-development spending up to $250,000 from payroll taxes in the following year instead of against income taxes.

- More flexible SBA lending: Make Small Business Administration lending more readily available, less complex and cumbersome, less physical-asset-based, and less restrictive for new businesses.

- New tax credits: Promote the formation and commitment of "angel capital" by enacting a federal tax credit equal to 25 percent of investment in a start-up and exempting from federal income tax capital gains on investments in start-ups held for at least three years.

- Exempt from compliance with section 404 of the Sarbanes-Oxley Act: Allow companies with annual gross revenue of less than $500 million to be exempt from this costly part of the legislation that requires management to produce an "internal control report"; permit companies with annual gross revenues between $500 million and $5 billion to opt out of section-404 compliance during the first five years of operation.

- Enhance market for smaller IPOs: To create a more robust market for small initial public offerings (IPOs), have the SEC create an optional pricing regime for shares of public companies with market capitalization of less than $700 million.

- Preferential regulatory framework: Have the Congressional Budget Office and the Office of Management and Budget co-develop a preferential regulatory framework for new businesses, subjecting them to only the most essential product-safety, environmental, and worker-protection regulations during their first five years.

Opportunities in Health-Care Reform

Since the passage of the Patient Protection and Affordable Care Act in 2010, health care has been perhaps the most contentious political debate in America. Both Democrats and Republicans have strong views on the law, and that isn't likely to change anytime soon.

No one can say with certainty what shape the law will take or what impact it will have in the years ahead. But in the meantime, there are steps that can be taken to further strengthen our health-care system and, by extension, our ability to create jobs.

Uncertainty about the Affordable Care Act is no excuse for inaction.

While debate on the law continues, the inexorable force shaping our health-care system will continue to grow stronger.

In a rapidly aging America—every day, some 8,000 baby boomers turn 65—more people will require more access to more expensive medical care.

The number of Americans 65 or older is projected to double, from roughly 40 million to about 80 million, in the next two decades, when they will constitute one-fifth of the population.[89]

According to the World Health Organization, in 2012 the United States spent $8,895 per capita on health care[90]—more as a percentage of its GDP (17.9 percent) than any other nation.[91] And health-care spending in the U.S. is projected to be close to 25 percent of GDP in 20 years.[92]

The Affordable Care Act has provisions intended to deal with both the access and cost challenges of health care, but it is certainly not the last word in reform. And while dealing with the growing demand for and cost of health care will be challenging, it is not without opportunity.

Effective health-care reform measures could have both a direct and indirect impact on our ability to create 25 million jobs over the next 10 years.

---

89 www.agingstats.gov/Main_Site/Data/2012_Documents/Population.aspx
90 www.data.worldbank.org/indicator/SH.XPD.PCAP/countries
91 www. data.worldbank.org/indicator/SH.XPD.TOTL.ZS
92 www.brookings.edu/about/projects/bpea/latest-conference/2013-fall-chandra-healthcare-spending

Direct impact: The simple fact that more people will need more health care means that more doctors, nurses, and other practitioners will be needed to provide it.

Indirect impact: About 149 million non-elderly Americans received health benefits through their employers in 2012.[93] So increases in health-care costs mean employers have to pay more. Conversely, any success in reducing health-care costs leaves employers with more capital to invest and to hire.

The twin goals of reducing costs and improving care depend in part on adding the right kinds of jobs in the right places—and providing the right kinds of incentives.

IDEAS: MORE HEALTH-CARE WORKERS, REDUCED COSTS

The American Association of Medical Colleges estimates that the U.S. faces a shortage of more than 90,000 physicians by 2020 and 130,000 by 2025,[94] with significant need for more primary-care physicians, internists, family practitioners, and pediatricians.

Besides encouraging more medical students to enter primary care, several initiatives in the Affordable Care Act are aimed at increasing the number of "mid-level" health-care workers—well-trained providers who can help doctors see more patients (and spend more time on serious cases) at about half the cost of physicians—through scholarship and loan-repayment programs.[95] These "mid-level" providers include nurse practitioners, physician assistants, community health-care workers, nurse midwives, and more.

Nurse practitioners and physician assistants have the skills to provide many of the tasks that primary-care physicians do, including performing physical exams, prescribing medicines and diagnostic tests, and diagnosing and treating such conditions as diabetes and high blood pressure.[96]

---

93 www. kff.org/report-section/2013-summary-of-findings/
94 www.aamc.org/download/153160/data/physician_shortages_to_worsen_
     without_increases_in_residency_tr.pdf
95 www.commonwealthfund.org/~/media/Files/Publications/Issue%20
     Brief/2011/Jan/1466_Abrams_how_ACA_will_strengthen_primary_
     care_reform_brief_v3.pdf
96 www.marketplace.org/topics/economy/health-care/nurse-practitioner-will-
     see-you-now

Provide Incentives To Expand the Ranks —and Services—of Mid-level Practitioners

Increasing funding for scholarships, loans, and other education and training incentives for mid-level and other health-care workers, such as diagnostic technicians and occupational and physical therapists, could help relieve the overwhelming pressure on primary-care physicians and pay off in terms of both increased care and lower costs.

A barrier to more extensive use of mid-level health-care providers is the fact that individual states determine the "scope of practice" that they can engage in. Increasing federal incentives for states to expand the "scope of practice" for mid-level health-care workers up to their levels of expertise and training could help increase access to good health care and lower its cost.

Reward Coordination of Care, Not More Services

The major thrust of current cost-reduction efforts is to switch the health-care payment model from fee-for-service to value- and outcome-based payments. This often means rewarding coordinated care through integrated-delivery systems ranging from accountable-care organizations to patient-centered "medical homes" to community health centers and other facilities.

The Affordable Care Act funds a number of programs testing various models for coordinated care, including primary- and preventive-care clinics run by nurse practitioners in medically underserved regions. Programs that prove successful should be replicated where settings and circumstances seem to offer similar opportunities.

Bring Better Care and Lower Cost to Medicare

Because almost 16 percent of the nation's population relies on Medicare for health-insurance coverage, improvements in its effectiveness have major consequences for the overall cost of medical care, the nation's health, our health-care system, and the federal budget.

The "Better Care, Lower Cost Act"—introduced by Senators Ron Wyden (D-OR) and Johnny Isakson (R-GA) and Representatives Erik Paulsen (R-MN) and Peter Welch (D-VT)—is a bipartisan, bicameral piece of legislation that focuses on improving care and reducing Medicare costs by promoting the use of multidisciplinary health teams to provide care for people with multiple chronic conditions in their homes and communities.

According to the Centers for Medicare and Medicaid Services, patients with multiple chronic conditions are the fastest-growing and most expensive portion of the Medicare population, constituting 68 percent of Medicare beneficiaries and accounting for 93 percent of Medicare spending and 98 percent of hospital readmissions. Any reduction in costs of treating chronic care patients could have a hugely beneficial ripple effect throughout the health-care system.

Under the "Better Care, Lower Cost Act", patients would voluntarily enroll in a program that offers incentives for health-care providers to employ innovative solutions for keeping them healthy, such as tele-health technology to overcome geographic barriers that impede care. Participating plans would be allowed to focus and specialize in chronic-care delivery and management. The bill focuses particularly on rural and other underserved areas that lack integrated-delivery models and where chronic disease is prevalent, and ensures that health providers in those areas would be able to offer the full array of services authorized by their licenses.[97]

Learn from the States

- Many states have undertaken innovative programs designed to chip away at the $400 billion a year they spend collectively on health care. The federal government might take a lesson, or several, from some of those initiatives and incorporate them into its own programs or encourage their broader adoption. Among those outlined

---

97 www.wyden.senate.gov/news/press-releases/bipartisan-bicameral-medicare-reforms-seek-to-improve-care-and-lower-costs

by the National Conference of State Legislatures:[98]

- Monitor prescription drug abuse. Insurance fraud costs public and private health insurers billions of dollars a year. Storing prescription-drug information in a database allows it to be monitored and analyzed so patterns of illegal use and distribution can be identified, thereby deterring fraudulent prescription-drug insurance claims and impeding black-market resale of prescription drugs. Many states also require patients to have a physical exam before controlled drugs can be prescribed and to show a valid ID when picking up prescriptions at a pharmacy.

- Expand information technology. The use of electronic health records can help reduce administrative costs, improve patient care, and reduce medical errors. The federal government has provided funds to help states and providers adopt or upgrade health IT systems. The benefits of technology include the creation of tele-intensive-care units that allow physicians to monitor hospitalized patients from remote locations.

- Promote healthy behaviors. Some 75 percent of all health-care costs go to treating heart disease, cancer, diabetes, and arthritis, according to the Centers for Disease Control and Prevention. Investing $10 per person a year in programs to increase physical activity, improve nutrition, and curb tobacco use could save the nation in excess of $16 billion annually in five years by interrupting the onset of these chronic diseases. Wellness programs generate savings to both public and private employers, including states and localities.

- Increase patient safety. Medical errors are costly—and can be deadly. In fact, they are the eighth leading cause of death in the U.S. and cost more than $19.5 billion a year. One source of errors: Doctors' notoriously illegible handwriting can result in patients' receiving incorrect dosages or even the wrong drug altogether. A widely adopted remedy is allowing—or even mandating—that

98 www.ncsl.org/research/health/great-ideas-for-cutting-costs.aspx

prescriptions be transmitted electronically, also known as e-prescribing. Many states also have laws restricting payment for "never events"—errors that result in serious harm, such as surgery on the wrong body part and hospital-acquired infections.

- Consider medical-malpractice reform. According to researchers at Harvard University, America's medical liability system accounts for 2.4 percent of all health spending. Limiting malpractice awards, reducing the number of claims through mediation, and promoting best medical practices could reduce costs and help patients. The vast majority of providers support models that disclose adverse events, apologize to patients or their families, and encourage mediation. Also worth considering are programs that provide adequate funding for investigating complaints and disciplining doctors, tracking medical errors and instances of malpractice, and developing clinical guidelines for successful practices.

- Help patients decide. If you have severe back pain, do you have surgery or not? Oddly enough, that depends in part on where you live—on whether physicians there are more likely to recommend surgery than those elsewhere. Such unwarranted variations in medical care might account for as much as 30 percent of Medicare costs, according to researchers at Dartmouth University. A relatively new strategy for educating patients about important health-care decisions—called "patient decision aids"—employs videos, pamphlets, and Web-based tools to present risks and benefits of treatment and screening options. Research shows that patients who use them tend to choose less costly and less invasive options.

Tying It All Together

America has experienced its share of economic woes before. But our rich natural resources, enterprising citizens, and guiding democratic principles have always enabled us to rebound with increasing strength and prosperity, even from the Great Depression of the 1930s.

Since the end of the recession more than five years ago, however, we've been reminded that economic growth and prosperity are not givens. This time, and in fact after every downturn since the 1990s, job creation has lagged further and further behind our economic recovery.

"The recovery still feels like a recession to many Americans," Federal Reserve Board Chair Janet Yellen said last spring in her first public speech after taking charge of the nation's central bank.

It's no wonder that when No Labels surveyed citizens about their priorities for this country last year, the creation of 25 million jobs over the next decade was cited by the greatest number of people, both Democrats and Republicans.

We may not be exactly sure why job creation is still difficult. As we've noted, experts disagree on the causes. But we know enough about the likely contributing factors, from flawed immigration policies to a decline in the number of start-up companies, to be able to suggest real solutions to the problem.

The possible fixes we've outlined in the previous five chapters come from a variety of sources: members of Congress and White House officials, past and present, from both parties, as well as economists, lawyers, educators, and policy experts. Their recommendations have been crafted with an eye toward boosting the economy and, in particular, job creation.

We know we can't look at the jobs problem the way we have in the past and depend on the same approaches if we hope to solve this problem.

So the menu of options you've just read about includes new solutions, new partnerships, and new roles for both government and the private sector. Today's jobs challenge demands this sort of creativity, along with a sense of urgency and the courage of our political leaders to embrace this critically important goal and then to act.

GOAL #2

BALANCE THE FEDERAL BUDGET BY 2030

REINING IN OUR DEBT STRATEGICALLY AND RESPONSIBLY

Where Your Tax Dollars Go:
The U.S. Federal Budget

Most of Budget Goes Toward Defense,
Social Security, and Major Health Programs

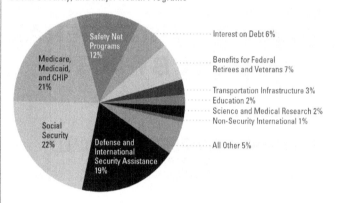

Safety Net Programs 12%

Medicare, Medicaid, and CHIP 21%

Social Security 22%

Defense and International Security Assistance 19%

Interest on Debt 6%

Benefits for Federal Retirees and Veterans 7%

Transportation Infrastructure 3%
Education 2%
Science and Medical Research 2%
Non-Security International 1%

All Other 5%

Source: 2012 figures from Office of Management and Budget, FY 2014 Historical Tables.

U.S. Federal Tax Receipts
Fiscal Year 2012 ($ Billions)

Total: $2,449 B

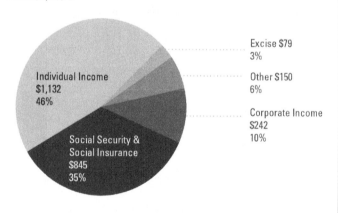

Individual Income $1,132 46%

Social Security & Social Insurance $845 35%

Excise $79 3%

Other $150 6%

Corporate Income $242 10%

Source: CBO Historical Tables

Balancing the Budget: Just the Facts

- Most of the federal budget—about two-thirds—is composed of just three things: defense spending, Social Security, and health-care programs such as Medicare and Medicaid.[99]
- The debt now stands at about 74 percent of GDP, which is higher today than at any time in U.S. history except at the end of World War II. It could soar to as high as 106 percent of GDP by 2039.
- Too much debt can lead to escalating interest rates on everything from mortgages to student loans.
- By 2024, the CBO projects that the amount the U.S. government pays in interest on the nation's debt could equal 80 percent of the cost of Medicare.
- The short-term bipartisan budget agreement forged by Sen. Patty Murray and Rep. Paul Ryan expires in October 2015, and when it does, America will be right back where we started: with government spending that will significantly exceed revenues for years to come.

The Problem:
America Is Spending Beyond Its Means

Balancing the federal budget isn't anything like balancing a household budget, and not just because the federal budget is a lot bigger. The U.S. government has the power to tax and to print money, which gives it much more flexibility and much more time to manage its debts. Moreover, the federal budget affects the economy in ways that household budgets do not. During recessions, revenues flowing into the U.S. Treasury shrink, but

99 www.cbpp.org/cms/?fa=view&id=1258

few economists believe that slashing spending to match this decrease would promote recovery and growth. When recoveries gather strength, revenues from individual and corporate taxes increase, shrinking the deficit. During expansions, spending restraints can promote growth by freeing up scarcer, more expensive capital for private investment, preventing interest rates from rising too high.

But the basic idea that government, just like a household, has to pay its bills and responsibly manage its spending and income over time is a sound one.

If the money we spend as a nation consistently outpaces the money we bring in, the burden of our increasing debt—including the interest we pay on it—will crush us.

Too much debt will eventually hurt the economy and make less money available to invest in infrastructure, research, education, and other building blocks of economic growth. The federal budget doesn't need to be perfectly balanced every year. In fact, budget deficits in the short term are manageable and in some cases can counteract recessions or fuel private-sector growth. America has run annual deficits every year in the last 40 years, except for the four years from 1998 to 2001.[100]

But we get into trouble when our debt—the accumulation of deficits year after year—grows faster than our resources and outstrips our ability to responsibly manage it.

Unfortunately, that's where we're headed. The federal debt held by the public is $12 trillion—and projected to get much bigger for a number of reasons, including an aging, longer-living population, rising long-term health-care costs, and a weak recovery from the Great Recession. But that $12 trillion figure is likely understating the scope of the problem, as America also has another $5 trillion in intra-government debt, mostly in the form of bonds held by Social Security and Medicare that will one day need to be repaid. That is $17 trillion in total that Uncle Sam has to repay to either public debt holders or to the public programs where promises have been made.

---

100 www.whitehouse.gov/sites/default/files/omb/budget/fy2015/assets/hist01z1.xls

Many Americans could reasonably conclude that $17 trillion is what our government really owes. After all, that's the gap that the U.S. government needs to fill to meet its current obligations.

But for the purposes of this book, when No Labels describes the federal debt, we are referring to the $12 trillion in debt held by the public. This isn't a No Labels endorsement of that figure. It's a recognition of the fact that much of the official budget data is predicated on the $12 trillion figure, so that is what No Labels will stick with to enable an apples-to-apples comparison of various budget proposals.

Even using the $12 trillion figure, our debt is still large and unsustainable.

The level of federal debt in proportion to our economy—what's referred to as the "debt-to-GDP ratio"— is projected to be at around 74 percent at the end of this year.[101] That's higher than at any time in U.S. history except for a short period after World War II,[102] and more than double what it was in 2007

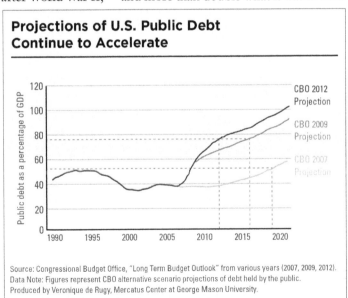

Projections of U.S. Public Debt Continue to Accelerate

Source: Congressional Budget Office, "Long Term Budget Outlook" from various years (2007, 2009, 2012).
Data Note: Figures represent CBO alternative scenario projections of debt held by the public.
Produced by Veronique de Rugy, Mercatus Center at George Mason University.

101 www.cbo.gov/sites/default/files/cbofiles/attachments/45471-Long-TermBudgetOutlook_7-29.pdf
102 www.theatlantic.com/business/archive/2012/11/the-long-story-of-us-debt-from-1790-to-2011-in-1-little-chart/265185/

when debt amounted to about 35 percent of GDP, roughly the historical average.[103]

The budget trajectory we're on is unsustainable. We ignore this warning at our peril.

The Stakes: The Downside of a Busted Budget

There's no consensus about how high a country's percentage of debt to GDP has to go before it becomes a problem. But the higher a country's ratio, the greater the chance that two terrible things happen:

1. Credit Gets More Expensive. If the owners of a country's bonds start to question that country's ability or willingness to pay its debts, they can demand higher interest rates. In the U.S., Treasury bills serve as a benchmark for virtually every other kind of debt, from mortgages and credit-card rates to student and small-business loans. Higher interest rates on Treasury bills eventually equal higher interest rates for everyone. Since the onset of the Great Recession, the Federal Reserve has worked to keep interest rates low, and owners of U.S. bonds have yet to demand higher rates. But these historically low rates can't and won't continue forever.

2. Debt Payments Diminish Our Ability To Make Other Investments. The interest we pay on the debt consumes hundreds of billions of dollars in tax revenues that could otherwise be spent on the urgent needs of our country—everything from job-retraining programs to infrastructure to emergency relief. Interest on the debt is money we have to pay off the top before we pay for anything else. The CBO projects that interest costs will nearly

---

103 www.cbo.gov/publication/44521

quadruple over the next decade as the debt climbs and interest rates return to more normal levels. By 2024, the CBO projects interest on the debt to reach about $880 billion, or 3.3 percent of GDP. That means interest will account for the bulk of the $1 trillion deficit projected for that year—and will equal close to 80 percent of the amount spent on Medicare.[104]

This debt burden holds the nation back and gives policymakers less flexibility to respond to unexpected challenges, such as economic downturns or wars.

How We Got Here

In the aftermath of World War II, the United States' national debt soared to 120 percent of GDP.[105] But this was a manageable challenge for two key reasons.

First, much of the debt was a one-time expenditure. Once the war was over, America didn't have to spend as much on all the tanks, planes, and other investments necessary to win the war.

Second, America's economy was mostly intact when hostilities ended in 1945, while much of the rest of the world lay in ruins. America's advantageous competitive position, combined with major investments in education, infrastructure, science, and technology helped deliver a quarter century of breakneck gains in economic and wage growth, job creation, and productivity. By 1974, our economy had grown fast enough to lower the debt-to-GDP ratio to a very manageable 32 percent.[106]

Today, however, America's long-term debt isn't being driven by one-time expenditures. It's being driven primarily by costs that aren't going away anytime soon like Medicare, Social Security, and defense. And America can't grow its way out of this problem because there is little reason to believe the country

---

104 www.cbo.gov/sites/default/files/cbofiles/attachments/45229-UpdatedBudgetProjections_2.pdf

105 www.blogs.reuters.com/great-debate/2013/01/14/why-public-debt-is-not-like-credit-card-debt/

106 www.theatlantic.com/business/archive/2013/02/why-the-us-government-never-ever-has-to-pay-back-all-its-debt/272747/

will be returning to its post-World War II economic growth rates anytime soon.

The CBO's projections show the debt rising over the next decades to 106 percent of GDP by 2039, and then even higher.[107]

The Right Way and Wrong Way To Balance a Budget

There are an infinite number of specific things America can do to reduce its deficits and debt and get our budget into balance.

But there are really only two approaches:

The right way and the wrong way.

The right way is what America did in the 1990s when both a Republican and a Democratic president struck a series of bipartisan budget deals that set America on a course to four consecutive surpluses by the end of the decade.

It began in 1990 when President George H.W. Bush worked with leaders from both sides of the aisle to fashion a budget agreement that included moderate revenue increases, spending cuts, and structural reforms. And it continued when President Bill Clinton partnered with House Speaker Newt Gingrich and a bipartisan coalition in Congress to do something similar with a budget deal in 1997.

The process certainly wasn't always pretty, and there was plenty of partisanship in the 1990s. Bill Clinton's first budget, which made an important contribution to deficit reduction, passed the House and Senate without a single Republican vote. But our leaders recognized that they had a responsibility to govern and to make difficult choices. They identified national priorities and made informed decisions about what was really worth spending taxpayer money on. In the major budget deals of the 1990s, some programs were cut because they weren't necessary or didn't perform as advertised. Other programs and priorities were expanded because they were essential parts

---

107 www.cbo.gov/sites/default/files/cbofiles/attachments/45471-Long-TermBudgetOutlook_7-29.pdf

of our social safety net or helped plant the seeds of future economic growth.

The upshot was a decade that ended with four straight years of surpluses.

That's the right way to budget.

When you budget the right way, you invest more in what works and cut what doesn't.

When you budget the right way, changes can be phased in gradually over time so government agencies, businesses, and citizens have time to adjust.

When you budget the right way, you actually have to make choices about what really matters, what sort of matters, and what doesn't really matter at all.

Unfortunately, Washington hasn't been doing things the right way for some time.

Instead of coming together around important national goals and strategically allocating resources to achieve them, Washington has lurched from crisis to crisis, striking eleventh-hour budget deals that either kick problems down the road or levy across-the-board spending cuts with little rhyme or reason.

The most notable recent example was the "sequester," a budget rule that imposed automatic discretionary-spending cuts throughout the federal government on March 1, 2013.[108]

It's worth recounting how and why the sequester happened because it's a perfect case study in approaching the budget the wrong way.

In 2011, Congress found itself at an impasse over the debt ceiling—which is a legislative mechanism that caps how much the government can borrow to fund spending. Congress has to periodically increase the debt ceiling to enable the Treasury Department to pay for already authorized spending. If the debt ceiling is breached, the U.S. government could default on its obligations, and the global economy would likely goes into a tailspin. It's not a pretty picture.

As the debt limit approached in late summer 2011, some members of Congress wanted the ceiling to be raised without

---

108 www.nwlc.org/resource/roadmap-2013-federal-budget-debates

conditions, as had generally been done in previous years. Others wanted spending cuts to be included with the debt-ceiling hike. On August 2, Congress settled on a compromise: the Budget Control Act of 2011.

This legislation raised the debt ceiling, but it did so with a key condition: A bipartisan group of legislators—called the "super committee"—would have to agree to a long-term plan to tame the debt. If the super committee could not agree, automatic, across-the-board spending cuts to government agencies and programs would be implemented after the end of the following year.

Here's the key point to understand: The "sequester" budget cuts were intentionally designed to be so undesirable to both Democrats and Republicans—by taking big chunks out of popular priorities like medical research and defense—that they would force the parties to compromise.

It didn't matter. The super committee couldn't agree on a plan, and the result was the implementation of the sequester cuts that most members of Congress never wanted to happen.

The sequester did at least have the virtue of helping to shrink short-term deficits. But it did little to deal with the long-term drivers of America's debt.[109]

In 2013, Congress passed a bipartisan budget plan designed by Senator Patty Murray (D-WA) and Representative Paul Ryan (R-WI) that replaced some of the sequester cuts and took a more strategic approach to funding our government.

But the Murray/Ryan plan expires in October 2015, and when it does, America will be right back where we started: with government spending that will significantly exceed revenues for years to come.

Now is the time for our leaders to start coming together around a real plan to get America's budget in balance by 2030. It will undoubtedly be difficult, and will require both parties to reconsider their entrenched positions.

But there is no other choice. Congress can act with urgency

109 www.crfb.org/blogs/short-term-deficits-may-be-shrinking-long-term-problem-remains

to deal with this problem proactively, and with a focus on stability and continuity in government and in our economy. Or Congress can have its hand forced by some future crisis, where it will have to make rushed decisions and immediate cuts that will hurt a lot of people.

Fortunately, there is already a bipartisan blueprint for action. Two of them, in fact.

In late 2010, the National Commission on Fiscal Responsibility and Reform (known as Simpson-Bowles for its co-chairs, former Republican Senator Alan Simpson and former Democratic White House Chief of Staff Erskine Bowles) and the Debt Reduction Task Force (led by former Republican Senator Pete Domenici and former White House Budget Director Alice Rivlin, a Democrat) released comprehensive plans to deal with the debt.[110][111]

The groups came to similar conclusions: Government needs reforms and reductions in discretionary spending; measures to tame health-care spending, especially in Medicare; changes to Social Security; and tax reforms that raise revenues without slowing economic growth. Both teams updated their plans in the last few years to account for changing economic circumstances.

The updated Simpson-Bowles plan seeks to reduce U.S. government deficit spending by $2.4 trillion over 10 years through a combination of spending cuts, health-care savings, and revenue raising tax reform. Along with previous debt-reduction deals and savings on interest payments, it would reduce the deficit by about $5.2 trillion over the next decade, enough to bring the debt to less than 70 percent of GDP by 2023 and below that in later years.[112]

Through a similar package of spending cuts, revenue increases, and reforms, the Domenici-Rivlin plan aimed to lower the debt to 69 percent of GDP by 2022 and 63 percent by 2032.

---

110 www.momentoftruthproject.org/sites/default/files/A%20Bipartisan%20
    Path%20Toward%20Securing%20America's%20Future.pdf
111 www.bipartisanpolicy.org/sites/default/files/D-R%20Plan%202.0%20
    FINAL.pdf
112 www.washingtonpost.com/business/economy/new-bowles-simpson-
    plan-aims-to-cut-through-deficit-debate/2013/04/18/9472b56c-a84f-
    11e2-a8e2-5b98cb59187f_story.html

It sought to cut spending by about $1.3 trillion by 2022 and $5.2 trillion by 2032 and to generate net new revenues of $1.5 trillion by 2022 and $7.6 trillion by 2032.[113]

IDEAS:
Getting America's Budget in Balance

There are three ways to make our debt smaller: Spend less, bring in more revenue, or grow the economy faster. Any plan for debt reduction needs to take all three of those factors into account.

The Simpson-Bowles report in particular offers a good starting point for discussing the broad options that are both possible and have some chance of winning bipartisan support.

Here is a menu of key budget-reduction ideas with the projected cost savings through 2023, along with some additional options and deficit-impact calculations from other sources.

CUTTING COSTS[114]

Replace sequestration with targeted cuts in discretionary spending. Savings: $385 billion

Congress enacted a series of measures in 2011 to bring down annually appropriated spending, including the Budget Control Act of 2011, which together reduce total discretionary funding by more than $1.8 trillion (including interest savings) from 2014 to 2023. The "sequester" cuts an additional $60 billion from discretionary spending.

This proposal would replace that across-the-board cuts with more targeted cuts. It would do so by:

- Maintaining 70 percent of the 2013 sequestration cuts; and
- Imposing caps on defense and non-defense spending through 2025 and limiting annual growth to inflation

113 www.bipartisanpolicy.org/sites/default/files/D-R%20Plan%202.0%20
FINAL.pdf
114 www.momentoftruthproject.org/sites/default/files/Full%20Plan%20
of%20Securing%20America's%20Future.pdf

as measured by the "chained" Consumer Price Index (CPI), which is able to reduce the CPI rate by accounting for the fact that people might respond to higher prices of products and services by choosing cheaper alternatives.

Adjustments to our health-care system under Medicare and Medicaid. Savings: $585 billion

Many organizations and interest groups have proposed an extensive array of adjustments to Medicare. Among the most comprehensive and bipartisan are the updated recommendations of the Simpson-Bowles commission, titled "A Bipartisan Path Forward to Securing America's Future,"[115]and those of the Domenici-Rivlin task force published in the Bipartisan Policy Committee report "A Bipartisan Rx for Patient-Centered Care and System-Wide Cost Containment."[116]

The policy options in the two reports vary in their details but share many methods and goals, especially their focus on moving away from the current fee-for-service system toward payments based on measures of quality and value, and on rewarding better coordinated care among providers.

For a look at some of the key ideas in these reports, see the chapter on Social Security and Medicare.

Cuts in other mandatory spending.[117] Savings: $265 billion

Though entitlements are the key drivers of the budget, reductions in other mandatory programs, which often rise automatically year after year, could be considered, especially since they're not subject to annual appropriations review.

Some areas for possible action:

---

115 www.momentoftruthproject.org/sites/default/files/Full%20Plan%20of%20Securing%20America's%20Future.pdf
116 www.bipartisanpolicy.org/sites/default/files/BPC%20Cost%20Containment%20Report.pdf
117 www.momentoftruthproject.org/sites/default/files/Full%20Plan%20of%20Securing%20America's%20Future.pdf

- Reduce and reform agricultural spending through a new long-term farm bill that restructures support programs ($40 billion);
- Reform federal workforce (civilian and military) health and retirement programs to more closely reflect pension benefits of workers in the private sector ($100 billion);
- Reform higher-education programs to streamline the numerous loans, grants, tax breaks, deductions, and credits currently available ($35 million);
- Impose or increase user fees for various government subsidies, such as those on public utilities ($50 billion); and
- Enact additional savings by restoring the financial integrity of certain institutions, such as the Pension Benefit Guarantee Corporation and the U.S. Postal Service ($40 billion).

GENERATING NEW REVENUES[118]

Reform the corporate and individual tax codes.
Gains: $585 billion

Most of the bipartisan proposals for reforming our complicated tax code involve reducing the size and number of tax expenditures in order to reduce the deficit, reducing the complexity of the tax code, and lowering marginal rates for individuals, corporations, and small businesses. The tax code currently features about $1 trillion worth of deductions and tax breaks. As some of these expenditures are reduced or eliminated, tax rates could be lowered accordingly. The Simpson-Bowles report proposes individual tax brackets of 12, 22, and 28 percent, and a corporate rate of 28 percent, while the latest Domenici-Rivlin plan calls for individual rates of 15 and 28 percent, also with a 28 percent corporate rate.

Credit Suisse offers these calculations for how much savings

---

118 www.momentoftruthproject.org/sites/default/files/Full%20Plan%20 of%20Securing%20America's%20Future.pdf

would result from the elimination of each of the following tax deductions:

- Employer-sponsored health insurance, $171 billion;
- Pension contributions and earnings, $138 billion;
- Mortgage-interest deduction, $87 billion;
- Accelerated depreciation of machinery and equipment, $76 billion;
- Preferential treatment of capital gains, $66 billion;
- Net imputed rental income, $51 billion;
- Deferral of income from controlled foreign corporations, $42 billion;
- Interest on state and local bonds, $39 billion;
- Charitable giving, $33 billion;
- State and local income tax, $33 billion.

For the full list, go to *www.businessinsider.com/the-top-20-tax-expenditures-2012-11*

OTHER CRITICAL BUDGET MEASURES

Adjustments to Social Security

Nearly one-quarter of our federal budget goes to Social Security. Like Medicare spending, Social Security costs are expected to skyrocket in the coming years due to the retirement of the baby-boom generation. Because there will be so many more beneficiaries relative to workers contributing taxes, the Social Security program faces significant challenges. Social Security's disability insurance trust fund is likely to be exhausted in 2016, at which point disabled workers could see an immediate 20 percent reduction in benefits. The old age and survivors insurance trust fund will be depleted by 2033, with retirees receiving only 77 percent of their benefits at that time.

Legions of analysts and policymakers—including the Simpson-Bowles commission and the Domenici-Rivlin task force, as well as the Congressional Budget Office, the American Academy of Actuaries, AARP, and the Social Security

Administration itself—have put together menus of options for making Social Security solvent in the long term.

See the chapter on Social Security and Medicare for a detailed list of options to change benefits or increase program funding, along with the percentage of the 75-year goal each would solve. These options include ideas from the Simpson-Bowles commission and Domenici-Rivlin task force, as well as from other sources.

For an interactive version and a detailed explanation of the proposals, go to *www.crfb.org/socialsecurityreformer**

Putting our federal budget on a sustainable path by reducing our debt is essential to our future prosperity and our role as a leader in the global economy. This isn't a choice between expanding the economy and reducing future debt. The two goals reinforce each other. We must do both—and we can. Doing so means coming together across party lines, looking down the road, and taking sensible action now for the sake of our future.

It's often said that we need to "pay for the government we want." But there is, of course, plenty of disagreement about how much government we want. A better way to look at the challenge before us is that we need to pay for the government we have. And if we think the government we have is too expensive, then we need to shift our resources accordingly.

It All Begins and Ends with the Budget

As we know, our budget is a lot more than a document of numbers in which column A, the money we bring in, needs to line up with column B, the money we spend. The budget, in essence, tells the story of our nation, how it works and where it's going. It lays out in very specific terms and details our national

---

*   Other lists of solvency options: Congressional Budget Office, www.cbo. gov/budget-options/2013/44750; American Academy of Actuaries, www.actuary.org/content/try-your-hand-social-security-reform; AARP, www.aarp.org/content/dam/aarp/work-and-retirement/social-security/2012-06/The-Future-Of-Social-Security.pdf

priorities and determines to the last dollar what our political leaders believe is worth collecting and spending money on.

So it's little surprise that budget debates in Washington have proven contentious through the years, crystallizing the ideological differences between the two parties and leading to ill will, gamesmanship and ultimately dead ends. It's little surprise that balancing the budget has proven so elusive.

But we know it can be done. Leaders who, in the past, recognized the importance of reducing our debt and balancing the budget, who put partisan grudges aside and worked with their adversaries for the good of the country, have shown us the way.

If ever we needed our elected officials to agree to this important goal and then make sure it gets done, it's now. A convergence of trends has sent us down an economic road that is unsustainable any way you look at it.

We have an aging, longer-living population that will be tapping into retirement safety-net programs in record numbers. On top of this, health-care costs are expected to escalate. And we've yet to fully recover from the Great Recession. That's a recipe for runaway debt, which in turn could limit our capacity to prosper as a nation—and as individuals—and meet the challenges of our global economy. That's too much to risk.

Our leaders must rein in our federal debt held by the public, currently $12 trillion and growing. That means taking a look at all of the options we've outlined above, from reductions in spending to entitlement-program reforms to changes in our tax code.

Our economic health begins and ends with a balanced budget. Once our spending and revenues are better aligned and our debt under control, we can reach higher, achieve more, and rest assured that America will have the ability to rise to whatever challenges lie ahead.

GOAL #3

SECURE SOCIAL SECURITY AND MEDICARE FOR ANOTHER 75 YEARS

SHORING UP THE SOCIAL SAFETY NET FOR THIS GENERATION AND GENERATIONS TO COME

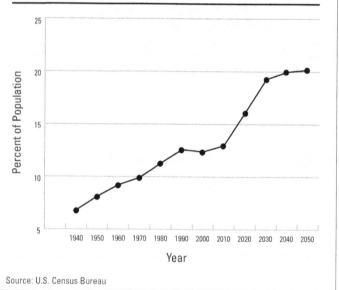

Age 65 and Older as a Percentage of Total Population

Source: U.S. Census Bureau

Social Security: Just the Facts

What It Does

- About one in four American households now receives a Social Security check. About 70 percent of recipients are retired workers; the rest are disabled workers and the survivors of deceased workers.
- More than half of all married, elderly, Social Security beneficiaries and almost three-quarters of unmarried persons receive 50 percent or more of their income from Social Security.

How It's Paid For

- Benefits paid to retirees and others come from two sources: payroll taxes collected from those in the workforce and their employers—the lion's share from the familiar FICA withholdings—and the Social Security trust funds, which hold any revenues that remain after benefits are paid out. If taxes fall short of benefit payments in any year, the trust funds make up the difference—as long as there is money in them.
- It's important to note that although Social Security accounts for about 22 percent of federal spending, it has historically been mostly funded by payroll taxes. Approximately 34 percent of federal tax revenue is derived from payroll taxes, which are used to fund Social Security, Medicare Hospital Insurance, and unemployment insurance.
- Congress has previously made adjustments to Social Security 10 times in response to demographic and social changes.

Why It's Unsustainable

- In 1950, there were 16.5 workers for every Social Security recipient. Today there are only 2.8 workers for every recipient, and that ratio will drop to 2.1 by 2033. At that time, Social Security benefits would need to be cut by about 23 percent.
- For many years, payroll taxes coming in exceeded benefit payments going out, and Social Security operated with a surplus, building up the trust funds to about $2.7 trillion as of the end of 2012.[119] But at current trends, the trust fund will be exhausted in less than 20 years.

Medicare: Just the Facts

What It Does

- Medicare provides access to health-care insurance for 95 percent of our nation's aged population, as well as many people who receive Social Security disability benefits. That's around 50 million Americans, or 15 percent of the nation's population.

How It's Paid For

- Medicare is funded primarily from general revenues (42 percent), payroll-tax contributions (39 percent), and premiums paid by beneficiaries (13 percent).

Why It's Unsustainable

- Without changes, Medicare funding for hospital expenses will run short by 2030, due to more enrollees, more expensive medical care and a reduction in the number of workers whose payroll taxes help support Medicare.
- Medicare cost $585 billion in 2013. That's expected

119 www.ssa.gov/oact/tr/2013/tr2013.pdf

to double to $1.02 trillion in 2023, increasing the program's share of the budget to around 18 percent.

- A typical two-earner couple would have paid $141,000 in Medicare payroll taxes during their working years. But under current benefit schedules, they can expect to get medical services worth $427,000—more than three times the amount they paid in.

The Problem: The Lifeline for American Seniors Is Fraying

Thoughts of retirement often stray to kelly-green golf courses, gardening, travel, spending time with family, and finally crossing items off the bucket list. But for many Americans, these dreams are often rudely interrupted by concerns about finances. People wonder what will happen once the regular paychecks are replaced by monthly Social Security checks—at a fraction of one's average salary in the workforce—and what will happen if or when we get sick. We know that the older we get, the more health-care services we need and the more costs we incur.

That's why many older Americans view Social Security and Medicare as a true lifeline.

Medicare provides access to health-care insurance for 95 percent of our nation's aged population, as well as many people who receive disability benefits.[120] Among elderly Social Security beneficiaries, more than half of all married couples and almost three-quarters of unmarried people receive 50 percent or more of their income from the program.[121]

But these lifelines are fraying.

These social insurance programs are in trouble due to a number of demographic, social, and economic changes. And our leaders in Washington will very soon have to deal with this problem by reconciling two often competing but essential priorities.

120 www.ssa.gov/policy/docs/statcomps/supplement/2013/medicare.html
121 www.ssa.gov/policy/docs/statcomps/supplement/2013/oasdi.html

We must, on the one hand, provide the benefits that our seniors have earned and depend on for a growing share of their medical and living expenses.

On the other hand, we must stabilize the government's long-term finances, and there is no realistic way to do so without reforming the way we currently fund and provide benefits through Medicare and Social Security.

It's easy to see why the debate over the future of Medicare and Social Security has been among the most contentious and intractable in Washington. Around 50 million people are enrolled in Medicare[122] and more than 58 million receive Social Security benefits.[123] Most people who work, as well as their employers pay into these programs.

So it's fair to say that any significant changes in Medicare or Social Security will affect us all.

But changes are exactly what are required. The simple fact is that Social Security and Medicare are not sustainable on their current trajectories. That's because of three epic trends: the retirement of the enormous baby-boom generation, falling birth rates, and rising health-care costs.

There are, in short, more Americans who will need more expensive benefits and a shrinking ratio of workers available to pay for them.

The nature of the problem is simple. Finding a solution to that problem is not.

But for the sake of this generation and the next, we have to try.

The Stakes:
A Problem That Can't Be Ignored

Together, Social Security and Medicare account for 38 percent of all federal spending—a share that is projected to grow as more Americans retire and collect benefits.[124] There will be

122 www.kff.org/medicare/state-indicator/total-medicare-beneficiaries/
123 www.ssa.gov/oact/progdata/icpGraph.html
124 www.pgpf.org/budget-explainer/medicare#1

more elderly consumers of health care, and that health care is becoming a lot more expensive. Between 1975 and 2010, Medicare enrollment doubled to 47 million, and the real cost per person quadrupled, according to the Centers for Medicare and Medicaid Services. By 2040, Medicare is projected to cover 88 million enrollees—about 40 million more than it does now.[125]

And most of these enrollees will be drawing more benefits than they paid in taxes. According to the Urban Institute, a two-earner couple—each receiving an average wage of $44,800—retiring in 2015 will pay $591,000 in lifetime Social Security and Medicare taxes and receive $935,000 in lifetime benefits.[126]

The imbalance is especially acute in Medicare. As a consequence, the portion of the federal budget consumed by Medicare will continue to grow—from 14 percent in 2013 to almost one-fifth of federal spending by 2040.[127]

Social Security and Medicare don't function like traditional bank accounts, where the money you put in belongs to you and is returned to you, generally with interest. In the Social Security system, the money you pay in is immediately paid out to those currently receiving benefits or placed in one of the Social Security trust funds that are supposed to help pay future benefits. Likewise, the checks you receive when you retire are financed primarily by those in the workforce at the time.

That system works fine if the number of people paying into the system substantially exceeds the number of people receiving benefits, as has been the case for most of the years since Social Security began in 1935. But the ratio of workers to retirees is dwindling so rapidly that the Social Security trust funds—which invest their surplus contributions in U.S. Treasury bonds—are projected to be depleted by 2033.[128] And that understates the problem, as Congress has actually been borrowing from the trust funds to pay for general annual spending to the tune of over $2 trillion.[129] Eventually, that borrowing will need to be repaid.

125 www.money.cnn.com/2011/09/05/news/economy/national_debt_spending/
126 www.urban.org/UploadedPDF/412945-Social-Security-and-Medicare-Taxes-and-Benefits-over-a-Lifetime.pdf
127 www.pgpf.org/budget-explainer/medicare
128 www.ssa.gov/oact/tr/2013/tr2013.pdf
129 www.nbcpolitics.nbcnews.com/_news/2012/04/23/11355323-social-

As for Medicare, its hospital insurance fund, commonly referred to as Part A, is on track to exhaust its assets by around 2030.[130]

Something has to give if we want to continue providing adequate benefits to older Americans, avoid burdening younger workers who have to save for their own later years, and keep from running up America's national debt.

These are not problems for future generations. This is happening now. We can't afford to ignore the fact that the bedrock of our social contract is crumbling—especially when we have the ability fix it.

Here's a quick look at the history and facts about each of these vital programs—and at the various tools at our disposal for securing them for the next 75 years.

Social Security: How We Got Here

When Social Security was enacted almost eight decades ago, America was a much different country. In the midst of the Great Depression, with unemployment around 25 percent[131] and two million men wandering the country as "hobos,"[132] Franklin Roosevelt proposed—and Congress enacted—an array of jobs and welfare programs: the CCC (Civilian Conservation Corps), WPA (Works Progress Administration), and a host of other agencies.

But Roosevelt also took a longer-range view of the nation's needs and championed the idea, already in effect throughout much of Europe, of replacing welfare assistance for the elderly with a program of social insurance. (FDR's distant cousin and presidential predecessor, Theodore Roosevelt, had advocated just such a program 23 years earlier.)[133]

security-trustees-see-earlier-fund-depletion-date?lite
130 www.marketwatch.com/story/medicare-trust-funds-life-extended-by-four-years-2014-07-28
131 www.fraser.stlouisfed.org/docs/meltzer/maremp93.pdf
132 www.books.google.com/books?id=JvKKjKL3nQcC&printsec=frontcover#v=onepage&q&f=false
133 www.ssa.gov/history/trinfo.html

The social insurance program FDR proposed was quite different from the short-term jobs and welfare programs of the Great Depression. It would address the perennial problem of economic insecurity among the elderly by creating a work-related, contributory system in which workers would pay taxes while employed in order to be assured of basic economic security later in life.

The Social Security Act of 1935 created a social insurance program designed to provide retired workers age 65 or older a continuing income. Originally, retirement benefits went only to the primary worker when he or she retired. In the years since, benefits have been broadened to include spouses, dependents, disabled workers, and others.

Of course, that's not all that has changed. Since the first monthly retirement benefits were distributed in 1940, America has undergone a seismic demographic shift. When Social Security began, the average life expectancy was 64. Now, the average life expectancy is 78; today's retirees, who can start drawing benefits at age 62, will spend, on average, 20 years in retirement.[134]

Through the years, Social Security has become—as the Simpson-Bowles commission put it—the "keystone of the American social safety net." About one in four households receives Social Security benefits today. About 70 percent of those benefits go to retired workers and their families, and the rest go to disabled workers and survivors of deceased workers.[135]

In 2014, more than 58 million Americans will receive about $845 billion in Social Security benefits,[136] including nine out of ten Americans 65 or older. Social Security remains the major source of income for the majority of America's elderly.

Clearly, Social Security is crucial to ensuring the economic security of tens of millions of Americans and their families. But with 8,000 baby boomers retiring every day[137] and many of them drawing Social Security benefits, the program as it's

---

134 www.ssa.gov/history/reports/ObamaFiscal/SocialSecurityProposals.pdf
135 www.ssa.gov/history/reports/ObamaFiscal/SocialSecurityProposals.pdf
136 www.cbo.gov/sites/default/files/cbofiles/attachments/45229-UpdatedBudgetProjections_2.pdf
137 www.aarp.org/personal-growth/transitions/boomers_65/

currently designed is becoming unsustainable.

In 1940, there were 42 workers for every Social Security beneficiary. In 1950, there were 16 workers for every retiree.[138] Today, there are only 2.8 workers per beneficiary, and by 2033—when the number of older Americans will reach 77 million, compared to 46.6 million today—there will be only 2.1 workers per beneficiary.[139]

In response to societal changes through the decades, Congress has made major adjustments to the Social Security system no fewer than ten times—adding classes of beneficiaries, increasing benefits, raising taxes, and changing ages and conditions of eligibility.[140] In the 1940s, Social Security was financed by a payroll tax of 2 percent; today, as a result of those changes, the payroll tax is 12.4 percent (half paid by employers).[141]

If the Social Security system is to keep its promise to the millions of Americans who currently rely on it and to the even greater number whose future well-being depends on it, another round of changes must be made. Without adjustments, revenues will not keep pace with expenditures, and the Social Security trust funds will be drawn steadily down until they are fully exhausted in 2033. If that happened, all beneficiaries would face an immediate 23 percent across-the-board benefit cut.[142]

But we can avoid that drastic 23 percent—which would be calamitous for millions of Americans—by developing a plan now that can put Social Security on sounder footing in the decades ahead.

Many ideas for doing so have been proposed. At the extremes, you could make Social Security whole just by significantly raising taxes or significantly cutting benefits. But those are options with little support.

Instead, there are a number of relatively modest and gradual changes to how benefits are paid and how the program is funded that together can help America reach the goal of

---

138 www.ssa.gov/history/reports/ObamaFiscal/SocialSecurityProposals.pdf
139 www.ssa.gov/news/press/basicfact.html
140 www.ssa.gov/history/briefhistory3.html
141 www.taxpolicycenter.org/taxfacts/content/pdf/ssrate_historical.pdf
142 www.ssa.gov/oact/tr/2013/tr2013.pdf

shoring up Social Security for the next 75 years. Here is a look at the options.

IDEAS: Options for Making Social Security Truly Secure

Legions of analysts and policymakers—including the Simpson-Bowles commission[143] and the Domenici-Rivlin task force,[144] as well as the Congressional Budget Office,[145] the American Academy of Actuaries,[146] AARP,[147] and the Social Security Administration itself[148]—have developed menus of options for making Social Security solvent in the long term.

Below is a list of options to change benefits or increase program funding, along with the percentage of the 75-year goal each would solve. These options, formulated by the Committee for a Responsible Budget, include ideas from the Simpson-Bowles and Domenici-Rivlin commissions, as well as from other sources.

For an interactive version and a detailed explanation of the proposals, go to *www.crfb.org/socialsecurityreformer.**

REVENUE CHANGES

1. Increase the payroll tax across the board:
   a) By 1 percentage point
      Percent of solvency gap closed: 38
   b) By 1.8 percentage points

143 www.ssa.gov/history/reports/ObamaFiscal/SocialSecurityProposals.pdf
144 www.bipartisanpolicy.org/sites/default/files/D-R%20Plan%202.0%20FINAL.pdf
145 www.cbo.gov/budget-options/2013/44700
146 www.actuary.org/pdf/socialsecurity/reform_07.pdf
147 www.aarp.org/content/dam/aarp/work-and-retirement/social-security/2012-06/The-Future-Of-Social-Security.pdf
148 www.ssa.gov/oact/solvency/
* Other lists of solvency options: Congressional Budget Office, www.cbo.gov/budget-options/2013/44750; American Academy of Actuaries, www.actuary.org/content/try-your-hand-social-security-reform; AARP, www.aarp.org/content/dam/aarp/work-and-retirement/social-security/2012-06/The-Future-Of-Social-Security.pdf

Percent of solvency gap closed: 68
  c) By 2.6 percentage points
    Percent of solvency gap closed: 99

2. Raise the cap on wages subject to the Social Security tax:
  a) To cover all wages rather than just the first roughly $114,000, the current cap
    Percent of solvency gap closed: 77
  b) To cover 90 percent of wages
    Percent of solvency gap closed: 32

3. Raise additional revenues by:
  a) Bringing newly hired state and local workers into the system
    Percent of solvency gap closed: 9
  b) Applying the Social Security tax to all salary-reduction "cafeteria" plans
    Percent of solvency gap closed: 9
  c) Taxing Social Security benefits the same as pension benefits
    Percent of solvency gap closed: 11

BENEFIT CHANGES

1. Marginally reduce initial benefits for future recipients by varying the ways annual pre-retirement earnings are indexed:
  a) Initial Social Security benefits are calculated through a formula based on average lifetime wages. This option would continue doing so for the bottom 30 percent of earners, would index them to the (typically lower) average increase in prices for the highest earners, and would index at a hybrid rate for those in between.
    Percent of solvency gap closed: 56
  b) This option (reflecting the recommendation of the Simpson-Bowles commission) would gradually alter the formula to reduce initial benefits for the

top half of earners by 2050.
Percent of solvency gap closed: 38

c) This option (reflecting the 2010 recommendation of the Domenici-Rivlin task force) would alter the formula to eventually reduce future initial benefits for the top 20 percent of earners.
Percent of solvency gap closed: 3

2. Gradually increase the normal retirement age:

a) From 67 to 68.
Percent of solvency gap closed: 13

b) Index benefit payments to longevity—that is, reduce monthly benefits to account for increase in projected life span—when the retirement age reaches 67.
Percent of solvency gap closed: 18

c) Raise to 69 and index for longevity.
Percent of solvency gap closed: 39

3. Change cost-of-living adjustments (COLA) by using:

a) "Chained CPI"*
Percent of solvency gap closed: 21

b) CPI–1 percent
Percent of solvency gap closed: 63

4. Calculate benefits based on the top 38 years of earnings instead of the top 35 years, which would reduce the average.
Percent of solvency gap closed: 12

5. Create a minimum benefit of 125 percent of poverty to protect retirees who were low-income workers and whose benefit levels were below the poverty line.
Percent of solvency gap closed: –5

Medicare: Where We've Been

In 1965 President Johnson signed into law historic legislation creating a new social insurance program that, for the first time in America, guaranteed health-care coverage to all citizens age

* "Chained CPI" refers to an inflation measure that typically leads to a lower rise in benefits over time compared to the present COLAs

65 or older. As LBJ said in a special message to Congress on the subject of the proposed program, "Compassion and reason dictate that this logical extension of our proven social security system will supply the prudent, feasible, and dignified way to free the aged from the fear of financial hardship in the event of illness."[149]

When Medicare rolled out the following year, some 19 million Americans[150]—just under one-tenth of the population[151]—signed up. With significant expansions of the program enacted in the years since, Medicare now helps beneficiaries pay for hospital and physician visits, prescription drugs, and other important health services.

Today, around 50 million elderly and disabled Americans— almost 16 percent of the nation's population[152]—rely on Medicare for their health-insurance coverage. And with increasing life expectancies—and some 8,000 baby boomers turning 65 every day—the number of people enrolled in Medicare is expected to reach nearly 80 million by 2030.[153]

Medicare is a crucial piece of America's social safety net— and one of the most costly. As more beneficiaries consume more expensive medical services, the amount spent on Medicare is expected to nearly double in the next decade, from $585 billion in 2013 to $1.02 trillion in 2023.[154] According to the Medicare Actuary, the program will grow from 3.6 percent of the nation's GDP in 2010 to 6.5 percent by 2087.[155]

Medicare is funded primarily from general revenues (42 percent), payroll-tax contributions (39 percent), and premiums paid by beneficiaries (13 percent).[156] Higher-income taxpayers pay higher payroll taxes into the program, and higher-income beneficiaries pay a larger share of their health-care costs than

149 www.ssa.gov/history/briefhistory3.html
150 www.ssa.gov/history/ssa/lbjmedicare3.html
151 www.census.gov/population/estimates/nation/popclockest.txt
152 www.census.gov/popclock/
153 www.aarp.org/content/dam/aarp/research/public_policy_institute/health/who-relies-on-medicare-factsheet-AARP-ppi-health.pdf
154 www.cbo.gov/sites/default/files/cbofiles/attachments/45229-UpdatedBudgetProjections_2.pdf
155 www.downloads.cms.gov/files/TR2013.pdf
156 www.pgpf.org/Issues-In-Brief/who-pays-for-medicare-10042012

lower-income participants. In fact, the majority of beneficiaries pay substantial out-of-pocket costs—one in four spends 30 percent or more of their income on health expenses.[157]

Medicare consists of four parts, Part A (hospital insurance), Part B (medical insurance), Part C (private insurance plans such as Medicare Advantage that are approved by Medicare), and Part D (private insurance plans that offer prescription drug coverage).[158] Medicare Part A is the vulnerable part of Medicare because it is funded through a trust fund arrangement. Parts B, C and D are required by law to be adequately funded every year.

Medicare Part A faces an even greater challenge than Social Security: not only are more people living longer, but they are also consuming increasingly expensive medical services.

In recent years, health-care costs have increased at a rate greater than inflation. Despite a decrease in costs since the onset of the Great Recession, the upward cost trend is expected to resume as the economy gets stronger and new medical treatments become available. Between 2012 and 2023, Medicare's share of the federal budget is expected to increase from 13.2 percent to 14.7 percent.[159]

For much of the last 50 years, health-care spending per person has risen on average 2.5 percent faster than GDP.[160] The increase has been driven primarily by two factors, one good and one not so good.

One is that more health-care services are now available, along with more advanced technologies and more ways for doctors to diagnose and treat diseases. That's a development we all welcome.

Unfortunately, the way Medicare is structured also encourages doctors and other health providers to offer and encourage patients to use many more health-care services than they probably need. As a fee-for-service system, Medicare encourages volume rather than value. This is one feature of

---

157 www.kff.org/medicare/fact-sheet/medicare-spending-and-financing-fact-sheet/
158 www.aarp.org/health/medicare-insurance/info-01-2011/understanding_medicare_the_plans.1.html
159 www.kff.org/medicare/fact-sheet/medicare-spending-and-financing-fact-sheet/
160 www.ssab.gov/documents/TheUnsustainableCostofHealthCare_508.pdf

Medicare—and of our health-care system in general—that needs to change.

To start rewarding value over volume and offer the best basic health-care services to our nation's elderly and disabled—while at the same time keeping Medicare's finances secure for generations to come—some adjustments, both in financing and benefits, must be made.

IDEAS: Options for Reining in Costs and Maintaining High-Quality Care

Many organizations and interests have proposed an extensive array of adjustments to Medicare. Among the most comprehensive and bipartisan are the updated recommendations of the Simpson-Bowles commission, titled "A Bipartisan Path Forward to Securing America's Future," and those of the Domenici-Rivlin task force published in the Bipartisan Policy Committee report "A Bipartisan Rx for Patient-Centered Care and System-Wide Cost Containment."

The ideas in the two reports vary in their details but share many methods and goals, especially their focus on moving away from the current fee-for-service system toward payments based on measures of quality and value, and on rewarding better coordinated care among providers.

The following options for reining in costs while improving the quality of care are taken both from the Simpson-Bowles and Domenici-Rivlin reports. One signature proposal in both plans is to limit per-capita spending growth among enrollees in federal health programs to the rate of increase in the gross domestic product + 1 percent.[161][162]

---

161 www.momentoftruthproject.org/sites/default/files/Response%20 to%20Common%20Criticisms%20of%20Simpson%20docx%20 pjw%20edits_0.pdf

162 www.bipartisanpolicy.org/sites/default/files/Domenici-Rivlin%20 Protect%20Medicare%20Act%20.pdf

PREMIUM CHANGES[163]

- Increase premiums for higher-income beneficiaries so that they would be subject to graduated, income-related premiums (savings: $65 billion);[164] and
- Change Medicare cost-sharing rules to simplify premiums, deductibles, and co-pays, protect against catastrophic costs, provide low-income protections, and discourage overutilization of care and the use of costly supplemental plans ($90 billion).

PAYMENT REFORMS[165]

- Reduce and reform post-acute-care payments to skilled nursing facilities, home-health providers, and others to bring them more in line with actual costs and value ($70 billion);
- Enact delivery-system and payment changes to move away from a fee-for-service system and instead incentivize quality rather than volume through such measures as promoting participation in patient-centered network organizations and encouraging care coordination across multiple providers, and reducing payments in cases of preventable hospital readmissions ($60 billion);
- Reduce payments to hospitals by phasing out reimbursements for bad debts and reducing enhanced payments for rural hospitals ($65 billion);
- Reduce fraud, abuse, and excessive payments through such steps as validating physician orders for high-cost and high-fraud services, requiring prior authorization for advanced imaging, and further restricting and better monitoring physician self-referrals ($25 billion).

163 www.crfb.org/blogs/how-simpson-and-bowles-plan-bend-health-care-cost-curve

164 www.crfb.org/sites/default/files/full_plan_of_securing_americas_future_4-19-2013-9-30.pdf

165 www.crfb.org/sites/default/files/full_plan_of_securing_americas_future_4-19-2013-9-30.pdf

MARKET REFORMS[166]

- Reduce the costs of prescription drugs by requiring companies to give the same rebates or discounts for Medicare that they do for Medicaid, and by prohibiting "pay for delay," in which name-brand drug manufacturers pay generic-drug makers to delay putting their products on the market ($90 billion);
- Enact medical malpractice reform by, among other things, establishing a statute of limitations for malpractice claims, apportioning liability according to share of responsibility for injury, and applying a health court model in certain instances ($20 billion);
- Convert Medicare to a defined contribution plan as proposed by Domenici-Rivlin, in which traditional Medicare would compete with private plans on a federally regulated exchange. Limit increases in the federal contribution to the growth rate of the economy. Alternatively, reform the Medicare Advantage (Part C), the private insurance program in which 31 percent of Medicare beneficiaries already participate, to operate on a federally regulated exchange with a competitive bidding structure to lower premiums and limit subsidy increases to the growth rate of GDP.

ELIGIBILITY AND TAX CHANGES[167]

- Gradually increase the Medicare eligibility age until it reaches 67 in the mid-2030s while allowing income-related buy-in for those 65 and up ($35 billion).

166 www.crfb.org/sites/default/files/full_plan_of_securing_americas_future_4-19-2013-9-30.pdf
167 www.crfb.org/sites/default/files/full_plan_of_securing_americas_future_4-19-2013-9-30.pdf

Keeping Medicare and Social Security Strong and Solvent

Now we have the facts. The history. The conundrum we face today—and an array of options available to address them.

Social Security and Medicare are not just any government programs—they are foundations of our social contract and essential lifelines for tens of millions of Americans today and in the future.

That's why our leaders must figure out how to keep Social Security and Medicare strong and solvent for the next 75 years.

It begins with acknowledging the simple, unassailable fact that many more people are coming into these programs with fewer workers to support them.

Social Security and Medicare were designed in the early and middle parts of the twentieth century for a population with a different labor force, life span and expectations about retirement. It's time to bring these programs into the twenty-first century.

It's a daunting challenge, but as the menu of possible solutions outlined above suggests, it can be met through relatively modest changes phased in over a long enough period of time.

That's a lot better than doing nothing—and having Social Security beneficiaries wake up a few decades from now to find their checks cut by 25 percent.

That's not a place we want to find ourselves. And there's no reason to.

The means are within our reach. But putting them to effective use means we have to extend our reach—across the aisle, across political and cultural divides, across generations.

We've done it before, many times. And we can do it again. We must do it again. We just have to roll up our sleeves, look each other in the eye, extend our hands, and take the steps that must be taken.

Together.

Because that's the way we get things done here in America.

GOAL #4

MAKE AMERICA ENERGY SECURE BY 2024

STRENGTHENING THE FOUNDATION OF OUR ECONOMY

American Energy Security: Just the Facts

1. 80 percent of U.S. energy is currently derived from fossil fuels.
2. America doesn't have a single energy system. It really has three—one providing electrical power, another fueling our transportation system, and another heating our homes and businesses. Each is affected differently by various political, economic, and energy market developments.
3. America's major fuel sources—oil, gas, coal, nuclear, geothermal, hydropower, wind, and solar—each feature advantages and disadvantages in terms of price, pollution, availability, and reliability.
4. Major investments in U.S. energy infrastructure are typically made with multi-decade time horizons in mind.

American Energy Independence: The Wrong Goal All Along?

In 1973, every American got a harsh education in the importance of energy to our economy.

When OPEC shut off the flow of Middle East oil to the United States, the effects were immediate and profound:

Lines formed around the block at gas stations.

Our government tried—and failed—to put price controls on fuel.

Still, oil prices doubled. Then they quadrupled.[168]

Before long, the whole world slipped into recession.

In the middle of the crisis, President Richard Nixon

168 www.history.state.gov/milestones/1969-1976/oil-embargo

addressed the nation and expressed a feeling that Americans had across the country and across party lines:

Never again.

The president said:

> *"We must set for ourselves this goal: We must never again be caught in a foreign-made crisis where the United States is dependent on any other country, friendly or unfriendly, for the energy we need to produce our jobs, to heat our homes, to furnish our transportation for wherever we want to go."*[169]

President Nixon's goal of American energy independence has been echoed, endorsed, and, to various degrees, acted upon by presidents and politicians of every stripe ever since.

Go to any political campaign rally in most any state or district, and you will find few more reliable applause lines than some version of:

> *"We need to get America off of foreign oil."*

It seems, on the surface, to be such a laudable and commonsense goal.

All it takes is one look at the headlines coming out of the Middle East to figure that America would be better off if we were using less fuel from places like Saudi Arabia and more from places like North Dakota.

And there's no doubt that producing more energy here in America is a good thing.

But more American-produced energy won't on its own lead to more energy security.

To understand why, you need to understand that America doesn't have a single energy system. It really has three—one providing electrical power, another fueling our transportation system, and another heating our homes and businesses.

Each is affected differently by various political, economic, and energy market developments.

The energy sources that power the American electrical system—primarily coal, natural gas, and nuclear—are almost all

---

169 www.presidency.ucsb.edu/ws/?pid=4208

within the country. Natural disasters and political events abroad do not typically affect the availability and price of electricity. The price of electricity in the past has been stable, and this will generally continue in the future, as the sources of power are plentiful.

But our electrification system has plenty of its own challenges. Many of our power stations are old and produce too much pollution, and our rickety electric transmission is vulnerable to disruptions and cyber-attack.

America's transportation system—cars, trucks, trains, and planes—is drastically different from our system of electrification. It is powered over 90 percent by oil,[170] a fuel that is freely transported and traded around the world and priced according to the global balance between supply and demand. Although America now produces roughly half the oil it consumes, American businesses and families pay a single price for oil, whether it comes from North Dakota or Nigeria. That price has been rising in recent years due to increased demand and supply interruptions from natural disasters such as Hurricane Katrina and war and instability in oil-producing regions in the Middle East and Africa.

Here's the upshot: No matter how much oil America produces at home, the gas price we pay at the pump will still be set by global supply and demand. That won't change until America becomes less dependent on oil (from any source) for its transportation needs.

The third major American energy system is the heating system for businesses and homes, which combines the characteristics of the electrical and transportation systems— relying on domestically produced and priced natural gas and electricity as well as globally traded oil.

So the energy security challenges to the heating system are a combination of those affecting the electricity and transportation systems.

With this complex and interrelated mix of energy challenges, it's clear that America's long-standing goal of "energy

170 www.eia.gov/totalenergy/data/monthly/archive/00351406.pdf

independence" is at best a partial solution.

America's real goal should be achieving true "energy security" by 2024.

What does energy security mean exactly?

It means having the energy our economy needs when we need it, at a price that is not subject to foreign countries' manipulation or natural disaster and with minimal impact on the environment.

There are essentially four steps America can take to achieve better energy security across the three major energy systems—electrical power, transportation and heating:

1. More energy supply from domestic sources, including more diverse transportation fuels
2. More efficient use of energy
3. More modern, reliable, and resilient electrical generation and transmission
4. More sustainable (less polluting) energy fuel mix

When a nation is truly energy secure, its economy has the flexibility and diversity of fuel supplies to withstand the unexpected but inevitable surprises, be it a shift in energy prices or supply, an environmental crisis, or an outbreak of war.

There are many different ways to achieve the goal of energy security, and one of the key goals of the *National Strategic Agenda* is to get a conversation started on how exactly we get there. We must recast the conversation from false hopes of energy independence to the more realistic and achievable goal of energy security.

In this chapter, we will explain how the U.S. currently uses energy and explore what the U.S. government can and cannot do to promote energy security.

NATURAL GAS: THE GAME CHANGER

In the decades since the OPEC embargo, America has taken many steps to both increase the supply of domestic energy and to more efficiently use the energy we have.

New on- and offshore land was opened for energy exploration and production.

Congress has passed energy efficiency standards for cars and trucks, buildings, homes, and appliances.

Federal, state, and local governments have funneled billions into mass-transit projects like subways, trains, boats, and buses.

Most important of all, the private sector invented, innovated, and found new ways to access deeply buried fossil fuels, to make nuclear power safer, and to harness the wind and the sun.

In the last few years, the U.S. has undergone what energy expert Michael Levi calls an "energy revolution,"[171] with the biggest changes to our energy systems since the 1960s, when nuclear power emerged and the environmental movement was born.

On the supply side, U.S. fossil fuel production (oil, coal, natural gas) is at an all-time high,[172] and the amount of electricity generated from wind, solar, and geothermal has doubled since 2008.

Meanwhile, America's homes and businesses are using the fuel we have more efficiently. The Bipartisan Policy Center noted that "over the last four decades, energy savings achieved through improvements in energy productivity [i.e., efficiency] have exceeded the contribution from all new supply resources in meeting America's growing energy needs."[173]

Of course, the most notable energy news of the past few years was a geologic gift that few saw coming.

Thanks to advances in drilling technology, we have been able to access vast reserves of oil and gas from previously impermeable reserves of shale.

Almost overnight, the energy discussion in America shifted from handwringing about our dwindling oil and gas supplies to triumphant predictions that the United States is on its way to becoming the "Saudi Arabia of natural gas."[7]

---

171 www.foreignaffairs.com/articles/139111/michael-levi/americas-energy-opportunity
172 www.aei-ideas.org/2013/04/energy-milestone-americas-fossil-fuel-production-in-2012-set-a-new-all-time-record-high/
173 www.bipartisanpolicy.org/sites/default/files/files/

The upshot, according to the International Energy Agency, is that America could be entirely energy self-sufficient by 2035.[8]

But more abundant supplies of domestic fossil fuels do not solve all this country's energy problems. Overseas events over which we have little influence can still trigger recessions in the United States, and fossil fuels burned both here and overseas produce polluting emissions that must be removed, processed, or stored to protect our health, property, and prosperity.

That's why our country needs a comprehensive, bipartisan strategic energy plan that is designed to meet the twin energy challenges we face.

1. The world needs a lot more energy in the future.
2. That energy needs to be increasingly clean to mitigate any effects of climate change.

Past predictions about energy supply demand and technology have very often been way off the mark. So any discussion about energy security needs to be leavened with a heavy dose of humility—and basic agreement on how the U.S. really uses energy now and how that can potentially change over time.

American Energy Use: Just the Facts—and a Few Reality Checks on Our Choices

Forging a path to energy security is an altogether different exercise than, say, securing Social Security for the next 75 years.

Fixing Social Security certainly isn't easy. But it is more straightforward.

First, Social Security is a government program. So the problems with that program can be dealt with almost entirely through government legislation or regulation.

Second, Social Security is a math problem, albeit an exceptionally complicated one. If America can balance revenues coming in and payments going out, then we can presumably make the program solvent over the long term.

Energy is different. Although the federal, state, and local governments play a significant role, the private sector is often the one discovering, generating, and transmitting the energy. Government sets the rules in the energy marketplace. But business is often the most important player in the game.

Finally, energy security is a tougher goal to define. As noted above, No Labels has identified the key planks of energy security as:

1. More energy supply from domestic sources, including more diverse transportation fuels
2. More efficient use of energy
3. More modern, reliable, and resilient electrical generation and transmission
4. A more sustainable (less polluting) energy fuel mix

But reasonable people can disagree about how much emphasis to put on each of these priorities.

As part of creating the *National Strategic Agenda*, No Labels will spend the next year convening a network of government, business, nonprofit, and citizen leaders to decide what energy security really means and how we get there.

But first, let's look at some of the essential facts about America's energy system.

80 PERCENT OF U.S. ENERGY IS CURRENTLY DERIVED FROM FOSSIL FUELS

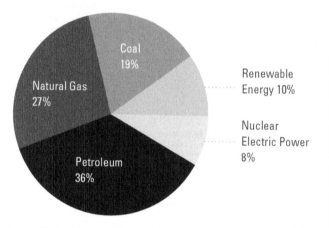

Primary Energy Use by Source, 2013

Quadrillion Btu and Percent of Total
Total U.S. = 97.5 quadrillion Btu

Coal 19%

Natural Gas 27%

Renewable Energy 10%

Nuclear Electric Power 8%

Petroleum 36%

Source: U.S. Energy Information Administration, *Monthly Energy Review*, Table 1.3 (May 2014), preliminary 2013 data.

THERE IS NO SUCH THING AS A "SILVER BULLET" FOR ENERGY

America is blessed with a variety of energy sources. The challenge is to figure out how to draw on the strengths of these sources while minimizing their weaknesses.

Oil is the most developed and efficient way to power the transportation sector, but it is traded on a global market, will probably become more expensive in the future, and leaves the U.S. economically and politically vulnerable to events overseas over which we have little control. In addition, as a fossil fuel, it produces pollution.

Natural gas and coal are affordable and abundant in

the United States, but each generates varying amounts of air pollutants, as well as the carbon emissions that contribute to global climate change.

Nuclear electrical power is affordable, abundant, and clean once a plant is running, but new plants are very expensive to build. All nuclear plants demand constant vigilance to prevent any release of radioactive materials, and a U.S. solution to long-term storage of used nuclear fuel has yet to be reached.

Solar and wind energy are clean but can be expensive, expansive (requiring lots of land), and intermittent. Although the costs of these renewables have dropped significantly—between 2008 and 2012, for example, the cost of a solar module fell by 80 percent[174]—there are still hurdles to their becoming a more significant part of America's energy mix. The sun isn't always shining and the wind isn't always blowing. Without significant improvements in electrical storage capacity technology and the national electrical grid, solar and wind can't yet be relied on for the scale of power that every utility needs to ensure the lights are on 24/7.

Hydropower is also clean, reliable, and usually affordable. But hydroelectric power plants can disrupt the natural flow of rivers, jeopardize the health of wildlife, and lead to environmental problems like erosion and landslides.

In short, there is no energy "silver bullet." Every single fuel source that America uses delivers real benefits, but every one also has trade-offs. That's why there must be a mix of options, so the country and local communities can choose the options that best serve the priorities of energy security.

CHANGES IN ENERGY USAGE AND INFRASTRUCTURE TAKE TIME

Energy is both one of the largest industries in the United States as well as the provider of the power that every other industry depends on.

---

174 www.foreignaffairs.com/articles/139111/michael-levi/americas-energy-opportunity

Energy is quite literally the lifeblood of the American economy.

Across the country—in the smallest towns and the biggest cities—there are hundreds of billions of dollars' worth of energy infrastructure that recover, refine, generate, and transmit the fuels that warm our homes and run our businesses.

America currently has almost 7,000 power plants,[175] over two million miles of oil and gas pipelines,[176] and 143 oil refineries.[177] Not to mention 46,000 utility-scale wind turbines[178] and 445,000 solar photovoltaic systems.[179]

What does all this disparate infrastructure have in common? It all requires a substantial amount of upfront investment and a long-term investment horizon.

That's why changes in the energy and utility industries take time.

A company that is considering building a large power plant, for example, will only do so if it's confident that the plant will be operating 30, 40, or even 50 years into the future.

With the aging of many American coal and nuclear plants, America will very soon have to invest in much more new energy infrastructure.

But it won't be built overnight.

Our nation has spent more than a century constructing the energy infrastructure we currently have. That's no excuse to avoid or delay whatever changes are necessary to improve our energy security. But it's a reminder that we have a long road ahead of us if we're to move from the energy system America has to the one we want.

---

175 www.eia.gov/tools/faqs/faq.cfm?id=65&t=2
176 www.phmsa.dot.gov/portal/site/PHMSA/menuitem.6f23687cf7b00b0f 22e4c6962d9c8789/?vgnextoid=a62924cc45ea4110VgnVCM1000009ed 07898RCRD&vgnextchannel=f7280665b91ac010VgnVCM1000008049 a8c0RCRD&vgnextfmt=printwww.eia.gov/dnav/pet/pet_pnp_cap1_a_ (na)_8o0_count_a.htm
177 www.census.gov
178 www.awea.org/Resources/Content.aspx?ItemNumber=5059
179 www.seia.org/research-resources/solar-industry-data

What Is Government's Role in Our Energy System?

The most contentious political debates in America all spring from the same question:

What role should government play in our lives?

So it can be difficult to discuss energy policy without addressing that foundational question of when government should step in and when it should step back.

For America to achieve energy security, we must at least agree that government has to play some role in the energy sector. There is no way around it. Energy exploration is often done on public lands. Most energy is delivered through public utilities. Energy infrastructure—pipelines and power lines—is regulated at the state and federal level. And energy extraction and production have huge environmental impacts.

Some governments around the world have more involvement than America in their energy sector. Some have less. But every government has some involvement. Energy is just too important to a nation's security and prosperity for it to be otherwise.

In America, recent history provides a few compelling examples of how government can play a productive role in the energy sector and how it can be counterproductive.

GOOD GOVERNMENT: THE IMPORTANCE OF BASIC RESEARCH AND BROAD STANDARDS

In July 2013, George P. Mitchell—the Founder of Mitchell Energy—passed away at the age of 94. In his obituary, the *Associated Press* called Mitchell the "Father of Fracking" and credited him with sparking the American shale gas revolution.[180] In the AP story, Mitchell's family described a "quintessentially American" story of someone who rose from nothing to become a great entrepreneur and energy innovator. Mitchell was indeed

---

180 www.huffingtonpost.com/2013/07/27/george-p-mitchell-dies_n_3662253.html

a trailblazer, and he deserved all the accolades he received. But he had some help.

From the federal government.

Although Mitchell's company came to market in the 1990s with a revolutionary fracking technique, it also drew on technology that was invented, funded, or subsidized by Uncle Sam.

To cite just two examples: Sandia National Laboratories developed the seismic modeling and imaging technology that allowed Mitchell to more precisely locate oil and gas reserves; meanwhile, the U.S. Department of Energy funded joint ventures that ultimately produced the diamond-tipped drilling bits and pioneered horizontal drilling techniques that were later adapted for commercial use by Mitchell Energy.[181]

In fact, Dan Steward, a former Mitchell Energy VP, told the nonpartisan Breakthrough Institute that "DOE [Department of Energy] started it, and other people took the ball and ran with it. You cannot diminish DOE's involvement."[182]

The lesson here is that government can play a critical role in funding the basic energy research that is too long-range, risky, or expensive for the private sector to handle alone. It's true in other industries as well, as breakthrough technologies ranging from GPS and the Internet to memory foam mattresses got their start in government research labs.

When government lays the foundation for innovation, and the private sector is empowered to build on that foundation, new products come to market, new jobs are created, and new solutions are found to old problems.

Government has also often found success in promoting energy security by setting broad goals—automobile, appliance, and building-efficiency standards come to mind—and then giving industry the freedom to innovate and deploy the best solutions to meet those goals.

As noted earlier, gains in the efficient use of energy have

181 www.thebreakthrough.org/images/main_image/Where_the_Shale_Gas_Revolution_Came_From2.pdf
182 www.thebreakthrough.org/images/main_image/Where_the_Shale_Gas_Revolution_Came_From2.pdf

done more to meet America's growing energy needs over the last four decades than new energy supplies. This was made possible not only by private-sector innovation but also by government efficiency standards that set ambitious targets for industry to reach.

BAD GOVERNMENT: PICKING WINNERS

In 2007, Congress passed and President Bush signed the Energy Independence and Security Act, which among other things required that gasoline producers blend 36 billion gallons of ethanol (up from 9 billion in 2008) into the nation's gasoline supply by 2022.[183]

At the time, both Democrats and Republicans touted the "ethanol mandate" as a solution to wean America off of foreign oil with a cleaner, homegrown fuel.

The intention was good, but the results have been dubious at best.

Since the law passed, the U.S. has reduced its dependence on foreign oil, but that has overwhelmingly been the result of new oil and gas supplies. Meanwhile, the ethanol mandate has had a number of negative unintended consequences.

Due to the mandate, as much as 40 percent of U.S. corn crops now go to ethanol production, which has ended up raising the cost of food for American consumers by as much as 5 to 10 percent,[184] and even more for consumers in poorer countries.[185]

Many analysts also believe that the ethanol mandate is contributing to higher gas prices[186] as well as damage to cars since ethanol is corrosive to fuel lines and engine parts.[187]

Even the environmental benefits of ethanol appear to have been oversold. An *Associated Press* investigation found that millions of acres of conserved land had been wiped out to make

183 www.epa.gov/OTAQ/fuels/renewablefuels/
184 www.online.wsj.com/news/articles/SB10001424052702303789604579198081681248494
185 www.aljazeera.com/indepth/opinion/2012/10/201210993632838545.html
186 www.nytimes.com/2013/03/16/business/energy-environment/ethanol-glut-threatens-a-rise-in-gasoline-prices.html?emc=eta1
187 www.reason.com/archives/2014/05/06/the-ethanol-disaster

way for cornfields.[188] And a 2013 report by the nonpartisan National Research Council concluded: "Although it may seem obvious that subsidizing biofuels should reduce CO_2 emissions because they rely on renewable resources rather than fossil fuels, many studies we reviewed found the opposite,"[189] due largely to the amount of energy required to produce ethanol.

The U.S. government has taken notice. In 2013, the Environmental Protection Agency actually proposed reducing the ethanol mandate by 1.39 billion gallons,[190] and there is a growing bipartisan sentiment in Congress to eliminate the mandate altogether.[191]

None of this means that ethanol is a "bad" fuel or that biofuels in general don't have a place in America's energy mix.

They do.

But the ethanol mandate—by trying to dictate a certain level of usage of a single fuel source—is a perfect example of the downside of government's trying to impose a simple solution onto a very complicated marketplace. And it once again demonstrates the folly of making energy policy decisions based on the unachievable goal of energy independence.

IDEAS: Achieving American Energy Security by 2024

If we begin with the assumption that the U.S. government has often promoted energy security basic research and broad standards that encourage private-sector innovation, and damaged energy security through overly narrow interventions in the energy marketplace, then there are a number of policy options at our disposal.

188 www.bigstory.ap.org/article/secret-dirty-cost-obamas-green-power-push-1
189 www.online.wsj.com/news/articles/SB100014240527023037896045791 98081681248494
190 www.desmoinesregister.com/story/money/agriculture/2014/06/27/ epa-ethanol-mandate-weeks-away-gas-supply-congress-renewable-fuel-standard/11447021/
191 www.tulsaworld.com/business/energy/sen-tom-coburn-joins-group-to-abolish-ethanol-mandate/article_d229c7e8-6356-11e3-bec0-001a4bcf6878.html

In particular, the Bipartisan Policy Center has developed an array of policy proposals in its recent report "America's Energy Resurgence: Sustaining Success, Confronting Challenges." Most of the ideas below are from this report, unless otherwise noted. This is intended to be a representative cross sample of policies that can give America more opportunities to achieve energy security by 2024 by spurring more energy supply and more diverse transportation fuels, more efficient use of energy, more reliable energy transmission, and more sustainable fuels.

There are, of course, numerous other policy options available. But the following represent many of the key choices and levers available to policymakers.

MORE ENERGY SUPPLY AND MORE DIVERSE TRANSPORTATION FUELS

Expand Access to Oil and Gas Reserves

Congress could expand access to oil and gas exploration and production in the Eastern Gulf of Mexico, and the Department of the Interior could accelerate the timetable for leasing areas off the coasts of the Mid- and South Atlantic states. Any new areas would be subject to a rigorous coastal and marine spatial-planning process.

End the Ban on Oil Exports

Some experts advocate allowing for the export of U.S.-produced oil, just like coal and gasoline are now. The move, supporters say, could lower international prices and make gasoline cheaper in the U.S. by incentivizing the production of more fuel around the world. More fuel supply from a greater number of producers could increase energy security by making the global oil market more resilient to unforeseen weather or geopolitical developments.

More Streamlined and Transparent Permitting for Energy Exploration, Transmission, and Distribution

Analysts on both sides of the aisle agree that the permitting and regulatory process for energy exploration, transmission, and distribution is too complex and opaque. Congress and the Department of the Interior could create a new commission to identify options for regulatory reforms as well as steps to create more litigation transparency.

Eliminate Energy Tax Expenditures

From 2010 to 2012, the federal government doled out $18.5 billion per year in energy tax expenditures, which are specific incentives given to promote the use of a particular fuel. To create a more efficient, transparent, and competitive energy market, Congress could phase out these expenditures over time, especially for more mature technologies.

The Energy Security Trust Fund[192]

This proposal, which has been introduced several times in the Senate Energy Committee, would redirect oil and natural-gas royalties from either existing or new production toward an Energy Security Trust Fund. This fund could support research into technologies that diversify fuels in the transportation sector, including: better batteries for electric vehicles, more rapid electric charging stations, and demonstration projects to stimulate and learn lessons from the introduction of electric, natural gas, and other alternative fuel vehicles into the transportation fleet.

MORE EFFICIENT USE OF ENERGY

Put a Price on Carbon

Based on the assumption that government should increase taxes on things we want less of (pollution) and reduce taxes on things we want more of (work or savings, for example), some

---

192 www.technologyreview.com/view/512571/obama-stumps-for-energy-research-through-trust-fund/

economists and analysts support putting a price on carbon. Versions of this idea include a carbon tax or a cap-and-trade system, where a market is created for permits to emit carbon. Under a cap-and-trade system, the number of carbon permits available is reduced over time (the cap), and companies can comply with the cap by either reducing their own carbon emissions or buying more permits on the open market from companies that are under the cap (the trade).

Some economists have suggested coupling a carbon tax with a broader tax reform effort, where revenue from the carbon tax is used to pay for reductions in personal or corporate tax rates elsewhere.[193]

The Energy Savings and Industrial Competitiveness Act of 2013

This bipartisan energy efficiency bill—sponsored by Senators Jeanne Shaheen (D-NH) and Rob Portman (R-OH)—is designed to spur the use of energy efficiency technologies in the residential, commercial, and industrial sectors of our economy. The bill was narrowly defeated in the Senate in early 2014. However, the bill features a number of ideas that have attracted bipartisan support, including:

Buildings

- Strengthens national model-building codes to make new homes and commercial buildings more energy efficient while working with states and private industry to make the code-writing process more transparent.
- Kick-starts private-sector investment in building-efficiency upgrades and renovations by creating a commercial building energy efficiency financing initiative.

Manufacturers

- Directs the Department of Energy (DOE) to work closely with private-sector partners to encourage

193 www.brookings.edu/research/papers/2012/07/carbon-tax-mckibbin-morris-wilcoxen

research, development, and commercialization of innovative energy-efficient technology and processes for industrial applications.

- Helps manufacturers reduce energy use by incentivizing the use of more energy-efficient electric motors and transformers.
- Establishes a DOE program—SupplySTAR—to help make companies' supply chains more efficient.

Federal Government

- Requires the federal government—the nation's single largest energy user—to adopt energy-saving techniques for computers.
- Allows federal agencies to use existing funds to update plans for new federal buildings, using the most current building-efficiency standards.

More information on this bill can be found at:
www.govtrack.us/congress/bills/113/s761/text

MORE RELIABLE ENERGY TRANSMISSION
Modernize the Electric Grid

The U.S. electric grid is aging and too vulnerable to disruptions. Most of it is also designed to deliver power from large stationary power plants at a time when smaller distributed and renewable sources are playing a more prominent role in electricity generation.

Utility and electricity transmission regulations are often implemented at the regional, state, or local level. But these entities also work closely with the Federal Energy Regulatory Commission (FERC). FERC could prioritize strategies and incentives to modernize the electric grid and enable investment in new, more efficient transmission and distribution infrastructure. One vital component of modernization is to reduce the grid's vulnerability to cyber-attack.[194]

---

194 www.bipartisanpolicy.org/library/report/cybersecurity-electric-grid

MORE SUSTAINABLE ENERGY

Investments in Carbon Capture, Reuse, and Storage (CCRS)

Carbon capture, reuse, and storage is a set of systems to remove the carbon dioxide from exhaust of power plants, use as much of it as possible for industrial processes, then store the rest. Currently CCRS is small-scale and relatively expensive—it adds over 50 percent to the cost of electricity.[195] More research, as well as proof of concept for large-scale demonstration projects, is needed to better judge the technological, commercial, and geological feasibility of carbon capture, reuse, and storage.

The Energy Department has previously funded demonstration projects, though the support has been inconsistent and one of the largest demonstration projects was canceled in 2008.[196]

The Department of Energy could fund more public/private efforts to develop and demonstrate cost-effective, commercial-scale technologies for carbon capture, utilization, and storage and begin developing a comprehensive, integrated legal and regulatory framework to govern long-term carbon storage. This also presents opportunities for international cooperation, as China, India, and all countries face the same imperative to reduce fossil-fuel emissions of carbon dioxide.

Investments in Nuclear Safety and Storage

Although the United States currently gets about 19 percent of its electricity from nuclear power,[197] no new nuclear reactors have been built in the country since 1996.[198] Though America hasn't had major nuclear-safety incidents since the near miss at Three Mile Island in 1979, nuclear safety continues to be a primary concern of the public.

To spur the adoption of more nuclear energy, Congress could:

195 www.vermontlaw.edu/Documents/Sovacool-et-al-EP-Coal.pdf
196 www.wired.com/2008/02/futuregen-clean/
197 www.eia.gov/tools/faqs/faq.cfm?id=427&t=3
198 www.eia.gov/tools/faqs/faq.cfm?id=228&t=21

1. Adopt an effective, long-term strategy for managing and disposing of the nation's spent nuclear fuel and high-level radioactive waste.

2. Direct more federal research to reactor safety and the development of small-scale nuclear reactors that could better fit into a more distributed and less centralized energy grid.

Increase Funding for ARPA-E

The Energy Department's Advanced Research Projects Agency (ARPA-E) funds high-risk, high-reward research into advanced energy technologies like battery storage, technologies for smart buildings, and various renewable energy solutions. It is modeled after a similar agency at the Defense Department, DARPA, which conducted the first research into what would later become the Internet.

Congress could increase the funding for ARPA-E.

More Energy Security Equals More Economic and National Security

One of the central ideas of the *National Strategic Agenda* is that so many of our national challenges are connected. Progress on one issue will inevitably lead to progress on others.

That's especially true of energy, which is the lifeblood our economy. It's no exaggeration to say that America could not have become the world's leading economic power in the twentieth century without access to abundant, reliable, and affordable energy.

Think about all the wonders of our modern economy, from cars and planes to computers and MRI machines. It's all made possible by energy.

It may seem obvious, but it's important to remind ourselves that energy is the essential foundation of economic and national security.

As you've seen in this chapter, energy security isn't just a matter of what kind of fuel we use or where it comes from. It also a matter of how we use it, transmit it, and deal with its environmental implications.

Energy security is a much broader and more important goal than energy independence.

And for that reason, it's harder. Achieving true energy security by 2024 will require our leaders to honestly assess and balance key economic and environmental priorities. Above all, it will require them to think and plan for the long term because our energy system will not and cannot change overnight.

Fortunately, America is blessed with an abundance of energy sources, and an abundance of talented innovators who for decades have been inventing new ways to better harness energy, whether it's buried underground, underwater, stored in an atom, or from the wind and the sun.

We have the resources. We have the talent. Now it's up to our government to develop the right plan, policies, and incentives to unleash them and make America energy secure by 2024.

PROCESS REFORM

To Make the National Strategic Agenda Work, We Need To Fix the Way Government Works

The evidence of dysfunction in and dissatisfaction with American government is everywhere.

Consider that our current Congress is on track to be the least productive in American history.[199]

Or the fact that public approval of Congress is at its lowest since modern polling began.[200]

The trouble isn't just with the institutions passing the laws, either.

The institutions implementing the laws aren't doing much better, with government agencies widely perceived as too inefficient and unaccountable.

In 2013 alone, it's estimated that the federal government made more than $100 billion in improper payments through everything from Medicare fraud to mistakenly awarded tax credits and unemployment benefits.[201]

Faced with this dysfunction, many Americans appear to have concluded that the biggest problem with our government is the people running it.

In one well-publicized poll in 2013, 60 percent of Americans reported that they would fire every single member of Congress if they could.[202]

---

199 www.npr.org/2013/12/24/256696665/congress-is-on-pace-to-be-the-least-productive-ever

200 www.gallup.com/poll/1600/congress-public.aspx

201 www.abcnews.go.com/Politics/wireStory/government-made-100b-improper-payments-24480504

202 www.nbcnews.com/news/other/nbc-wsj-poll-60-percent-say-fire-every-member-congress-f8C11374594

It's an understandable impulse.

But fixing our government will require a more nuanced response than "throwing the bums out."

Because the fact is that the people serving in government aren't always the problem. In fact, America's public officials and civil servants include people who are among the most intelligent, spirited, and dedicated you will ever meet.

It's not a popular perspective these days, but it's true. Most of the people working in government want to do what's right for their community, their state, and their country.

Unfortunately, our public officials and civil servants are stuck in a broken system that is governed by a vast web of outdated laws, rules, and procedures that can make it virtually impossible to get anything done.

Twenty-first-century America is a society that prizes speed, efficiency, and innovation, but our government bodies often can't deliver these things because they were conceived in the twentieth century and designed for a society with different needs.

No matter whether you want more or less government, we should all be able to agree that we need smarter, more efficient government.

And whatever policy ideas are embraced as part of the *National Strategic Agenda,* they will only be as effective as the government that has to execute them.

As Alexander Hamilton famously said in Federalist 70, "a government ill executed, whatever it may be in theory, must be, in practice, a bad government."[203]

Effective government is not a pipe dream or a lost cause. In the past, the U.S. government has risen to the occasion to win world wars, to send men to the moon, and to help spur the construction of an interstate highway system. And today, there are plenty of areas where the government operates with efficiency and effectiveness, including the safeguarding of America's water and food supply and the administration of Social Security benefits, to name just a few examples.

Some of the problems with our federal government are

203 www.constitution.org/fed/federa70.htm

a byproduct of inertia: Government does things a certain way because that's the way they have always been done. Other problems have just been deemed too difficult to solve, with lots of excuses for why "It can't be done."

But the American people and No Labels' growing national army of supporters aren't interested in excuses, and they have a clear message for Washington.

If there is a problem, just fix it.

In this chapter, we provide reform options for two institutions that simply have to do better if America is to achieve the goals of our *National Strategic Agenda.*

Congress and the federal bureaucracy.

Fixing the institution that makes our laws, as well as the departments and agencies in charge of implementing them, would make it that much easier to balance our budget, to achieve energy security, to secure Medicare and Social Security, and to create millions of good jobs.

The reform ideas that follow are taken from three reports: No Labels' *Make Congress Work!* and *Make Government Work!* action plans, and the Partnership for Public Service's 2013 *Building the Enterprise* report.

Though some these ideas may appear to deal with obscure practices or procedures of Congress and the federal government, they can have an outsized impact on the security and prosperity of our country and the potential of the *National Strategic Agenda.*

As noted at the outset of this book, No Labels is not yet endorsing any specific policy options to achieve the four key goals of the *National Strategic Agenda.* That will come after a year of conversation among citizens and their leaders.

But No Labels does endorse the nonpartisan reform ideas in this chapter, because we believe they will create an environment that is more conducive to problem solving and will increase our chances of achieving the goals of the *National Strategic Agenda.*

Fixing Congress

In this book, we have talked about the urgent need for Congress and the executive branch to tackle the big challenges facing our nation. But in recent years, Congress has struggled to fulfill even its most basic responsibilities, such as passing budgets in a timely manner and making sure government operates at a minimum level of efficiency and effectiveness.

One of the central causes of dysfunction in Congress is the breakdown of something called "regular order"—which is the set of rules, norms, and procedures that govern how business is conducted in the House and Senate. There are long-standing traditions in both bodies that are supposed to guide how issues are debated, how amendments to legislation are offered, how bills make their way through congressional committees and onto the floor, and how differences are reconciled between the House and Senate.

But in recent years, regular order has almost been abandoned entirely. Both parties have stretched and in many cases ignored House and Senate rules to gain maximum partisan advantage. They've done so at a high cost, as trust has collapsed among congressional colleagues and gridlock has stalled even such routine congressional business as confirming low-level presidential appointees.

In 2011, No Labels released an ambitious action plan called *Make Congress Work!*, which featured a dozen simple, straightforward proposals to break gridlock, promote constructive discussion, and reduce polarization in Congress. A modified version of one of these proposals, "No Budget, No Pay"—which links congressional pay to timely passage of the annual budget—became law in early 2013.

But the next Congress—which will be seated in January 2015—would do well to consider the full menu of proposals in *Make Congress Work!*, including our original, stronger version of "No Budget, No Pay," which can undoubtedly help make Congress a more productive and effective institution.

MAKE CONGRESS WORK!

1) No Budget, No Pay

Congress rarely if ever passes budgets on time. The result is more wasteful and inefficient government as Congress is forced to rely on temporary spending measures called continuing resolutions—which typically provide the money federal agencies need to operate based roughly on what they spent the previous year.

But this unpredictable stop-and-go budgeting creates havoc for government agencies and the citizens who depend on them.

No Labels believes that if members of Congress can't make spending and budget decisions on time, they shouldn't get paid. Every government fiscal year begins October 1. Under "No Budget, No Pay," if the congressional appropriations (spending) process is not completed by that date, congressional pay would cease as of October 1, and it would not be restored until appropriations are completed.

Although Congress passed and President Obama signed a version of "No Budget, No Pay" in early 2013, this version allowed member pay to be recovered once a budget was passed. No Labels continues to support the original, stronger version of "No Budget, No Pay," which would require timely passage of both the annual budget and spending bills and would not allow lost member pay to be recovered.

"No Budget, No Pay" is the only proposal in *Make Congress Work!* that requires a new law.

2) Up-or-Down Vote on Presidential Appointments

The Senate's "advise and consent" role on presidential appointments is critically important, but the process no longer resembles anything close to what the Founders intended, with too many presidential nominations held up with little justification.

That's why all presidential nominations should be confirmed or rejected within 90 days of the nomination's being received by the Senate. If the nominee is not rejected within 90 days, the nominee would be confirmed by default.

3) Fix the Filibuster

For most of the Senate's history, the filibuster was a tool to be used only rarely to protect the interests of the minority party. But recently, the filibuster has been used by both parties to virtually grind the Senate to a halt by requiring 60 votes for passage of most legislation.

In the first 50 years of the filibuster, it was used only 35 times. In the last two years alone, it was used more than 100. And senators don't even have to show up on the floor to explain themselves—just signaling their intent to filibuster effectively stalls legislation.

No Labels proposes a two-part solution to reduce unwarranted use of the filibuster in the Senate:

- **Require Real (Not Virtual) Filibusters:** If senators want to halt action on a bill, they must take to the floor and hold it through sustained debate.
- **End Filibusters on Motions To Proceed:** Today filibusters can be used both to prevent a bill from reaching the floor for debate (motion to proceed) and from ultimately being passed. If the Senate simply ended the practice of filibustering motions to proceed, it could cut the number of filibusters in half.

4) Empower the Sensible Majority

We need to democratize decision making in Congress to break the gridlock. If a bipartisan majority of members wants to get something done, it shouldn't be held back by party leaders who prefer to organize Congress into warring clans. That's why the House should allow members to anonymously sign discharge petitions, which allow a majority of members to override a leader or committee chair's refusal to bring a bill to the floor. A similar reform could be undertaken in the Senate.

5) Make Members Come to Work

Part of the reason Congress can't get much done is because

members are not showing up in the halls of the Senate or House more than a few days a week. No Labels believes Congress would get more done if both chambers adopted:

- **A Five-Day Workweek:** Most Americans put in a five-day workweek. So should Congress.
- **Three Weeks in DC, One Week in the Home State or District:** Instead of quick in-and-out trips home for fundraisers or hastily scheduled constituent events, members should have a full week available for working at home with constituents. They should spend the other three weeks in Washington, DC.
- **Coordinated Schedules:** A law can't pass unless it gets through both the House and Senate. That's why the leaders of both chambers should work to ensure their members are in Washington during the same weeks.

6) Question Time for the President

We should take a cue from the British Parliament's regular questioning of the prime minister and create question times for the president and Congress. These meetings may be contentious, but at least they force leaders to actually debate one another and defend their ideas. Here's how it would work: On a rotating basis the House and Senate would issue monthly invitations to the president to appear in the respective chamber for questions and discussion. Each question period would last for 90 minutes and would be televised. The majority and minority would alternate questions. The president could, at his or her discretion, bring one or more cabinet members to the question period and refer specific questions to them.

7) Fiscal Report to Congress: Hear it. Read it. Sign it.

The American people deserve to know what's really happening with our nation's finances, and we believe Congress should at least be able to work off the same set of numbers. That's why every year a nonpartisan leader, such as the comptroller general, should deliver a televised fiscal update in person to a joint session of Congress. The president, vice president, all cabinet members, senators, and congressmen must attend this fiscal update session and take individual responsibility for the accuracy and completeness of the comptroller general's report by signing the report, just as CEOs are required to affirm the accuracy of their companies' financial reporting.

8) No Pledge but the Oath of Office

One barrier to solving problems in Congress is that many members literally sign away their ability to do it by agreeing to campaign pledges from special interest groups that limit their flexibility to compromise or react to changing circumstances. It's time to cut the puppet strings that allow narrow interest groups to control members of Congress. Members should make no pledge but the Pledge of Allegiance and their formal oath of office.

9) Monthly Bipartisan Gatherings

Like any workplace, Congress depends on good relationships to function. When there are no relationships, there's dysfunction. To get members talking to one another, both the House and Senate should institute monthly bipartisan gatherings. The gatherings would be off the record and not televised. If both sides agreed, outside experts could be invited to brief members on topics of concern.

No Labels has helped make progress towards this goal by helping recruit more than 90 members of Congress into a bipartisan problem-solvers group that has met regularly over the last few years to discuss issues. Members of this group have also cosponsored legislation.

In July 2014, a formal problem-solvers caucus was formed in the House, the first group of its kind.

But we still need more members willing to meet more regularly with their colleagues across the aisle.

10) Bipartisan Seating

It's time to curb the cliques in Congress, where Democrats and Republicans too often segregate themselves from the other party. At all joint meetings or sessions of Congress, each member should be seated next to at least one member of the other party. On committees and subcommittees, seating also would be arranged in an alternating bipartisan way (one member would be seated next to at least one member of the other party) by agreement between the chair and ranking member. One option would be to arrange bipartisan seating in order of seniority.

In recent years, No Labels has organized efforts that have convinced many members of opposing parties to sit with one another during the State of the Union address. But this is only a first step, and Congress needs to make a more concerted effort to get members from opposing parties to sit with and ultimately work with their colleagues across the aisle.

11) Bipartisan Leadership Committee

Republican and Democratic leaders have allowed virtually every meeting to turn into a partisan pep rally. So they're the ones who need to help change the agenda to focus on solving real problems.

Congressional party leaders should form a bipartisan congressional leadership committee as a forum for discussing both legislative agendas and substantive solutions. The committee members would meet weekly and (subject to mutual agreement) also meet monthly with the president.

This committee would include the president pro tempore of the Senate, the Speaker of the House, and the Senate and House majority and minority leaders. It would also include four open slots for any two members of the Senate and of the House, which would be determined by lottery on a rotating basis each Congress.

12) No Negative Campaigns Against Incumbents

Sometimes we forget that Democratic and Republican members

of Congress aren't just political opponents but colleagues who actually need to build trust to work with one another. When members of Congress can't work together because of personal animosity, it's the American people who suffer. That's why incumbents from one party should not conduct negative campaigns against sitting members of the opposing party. That means no appearing in negative ads, no signing nasty direct-mail letters, and no traveling to an incumbent's district or state to play attack dog. Members would of course be free to campaign or fundraise in support of candidates from their party and against challengers from the other party.

For more information on the *Make Congress Work!* action plan, visit *www.nolabels.org/work*

Fixing the Federal Bureaucracy

Spend a few minutes digging into any of the specific challenges in the *National Strategic Agenda* and you are immediately struck by how solving one challenge makes it easier to solve the others.

Everything is connected.

If America's challenges are interconnected, our government's response to them should be coordinated.

Unfortunately, that is not how the federal government currently operates.

Too much of what our government does is siloed, with different agencies pursuing different or even duplicative missions. As the old saying goes, the right hand too often doesn't know what the left hand is doing.

To cite just one notable example, a March 2013 Government Accountability Office report found that the federal government had 76 different programs across 15 federal agencies designed to combat illegal drug use. Of those 76 programs, 59 showed evidence of overlap.

Congress and the president know that inefficiency, duplication, and lack of coordination are major problems for the federal government. To their credit, they recently passed the Government Performance and Results Modernization Act of 2010 (GRPAMA), which provides the basis for federal agencies to work together in a more coordinated fashion.

But this is just a foundation, and it needs to be built upon with real urgency.

BUILDING THE ENTERPRISE

In 2013, the nonpartisan Partnership for Public Service released a blueprint for how to do it.

The report, *Building the Enterprise,* suggested that "the federal government should act more like an enterprise, [which means] it should better integrate and unify the efforts of the executive departments, agencies, bureaus, and offices to achieve cross-cutting goals, missions, and functions the individual agencies cannot effectively tackle on their own."

Like *Make Congress Work!, Building the Enterprise* aims to "minimize the need for legislation or wholesale restructuring." *Building the Enterprise* recommends nine strategies to help the federal government take a more coordinated, multiagency, whole-of-government approach … to the nation's most difficult and enduring challenges."

Here is a summary of the nine recommendations:

1) Develop an Enterprise Performance Plan with Senior-Level Commitment to Drive Cross-Agency Goals and Missions

Under this plan, the executive branch would develop a comprehensive government-wide blueprint to identify the broad array of missions and functions that can best be achieved by a whole-of-government approach. It would include the necessary infrastructure and accountability mechanisms to increase the likelihood that targets would be achieved.

This plan should be organized around enterprise goals to include the program and policy priorities of the president, as well as enduring missions and functions of the government, such as assuring the safety of the nation's food supply.

Responsibility for this plan would rest with the President's Management Council (PMC).

2) Build Portfolios of Programs Aligned Against the Enterprise Plan's Goals

The idea here is to align and integrate all government programs that contribute to a particular goal (e.g., combating drug use, encouraging entrepreneurship, etc.). The portfolio approach will illuminate the strengths and weaknesses of existing programs and identify duplication as well as gaps. Portfolios of programs, not individual programs, will become the organizational approach to collectively achieve enterprise results.

3) Designate and Empower Enterprise Goal Leaders

Performance plans and portfolios are important tools to define enterprise objectives, but none of it matters without strong leadership. Building off of the GRPAMA legislation, the current administration has already designated goal leaders for each of its cross-agency priority goals, and those goal leaders are responsible for establishing governance councils and reporting on progress.

But the executive branch can go further by providing goal leaders with sufficient bureaucratic muscle over their program portfolios.

Specifically, enterprise goal leaders must be expected and encouraged to take a holistic view of their portfolios, independently assess the portfolio's constituent programs, and provide hard-hitting, honest-broker recommendations to the administration on which programs should be continued, expanded, curtailed, or eliminated.

4) Develop Career Enterprise Executives To Lead Crosscutting Missions and Functions

Thirty-five years ago, the federal government created the Senior Executive Service (SES) with the goal of developing a talented cadre of senior-level managers throughout the federal bureaucracy. But with few exceptions, these senior executives are agency-centric in experience and orientation, and as siloed as the government they serve.

This must change if the federal government is to operate like a true enterprise. Senior career executives must be developed with an enterprise perspective. For this reason, the Office of Personnel Management (OPM) should make interagency or intergovernmental experience and enterprise-leadership competencies mandatory in order to be selected for the SES.

5) Establish an Independent Office of Evaluation To Assess Enterprise Performance

Lack of accurate measurement is a long-standing problem for many government programs. Government programs and government officials tend to focus on the budget or the numbers of people served, but they are much less likely to try to link those measures to real-world outcomes.

For example, it is easy to document how much money is budgeted for a particular job-training program, how many training classes that money buys, the number of people who apply for or complete classes, and even the number who get jobs. But it is difficult to determine cause and effect (i.e., whether trainees get jobs as a result of the program).

A new Office of Evaluation should be set up within the Executive Office of the President or the Office of Management and Budget to conduct rigorous performance assessments that will determine whether programs are meeting their specific and enterprise-wide goals.

6) Manage Information Technology as a True Enterprise Resource

Today, the government spends $80 billion annually on information technology (IT)—$55 billion of it on operating and maintaining existing systems, the rest on buying and developing systems. Duplication is rampant, and opportunities for enterprise savings are huge.

The Obama administration has developed a shared-services strategy that directs agencies to begin consolidating purchases of IT services, which can often reduce the price of those services.

But this strategy needs to be much more aggressively pursued. The focus on enhancing IT capability should be expanded into a portfolio approach to all IT resources across the federal enterprise, not just within agencies.

This strategy should bundle shared IT services into portfolios (for example, an e-mail portfolio or a cloud portfolio) and designate goal leaders to maximize each portfolio's enterprise value, functionality, efficiency, and effectiveness.

7) Take Shared Services to Scale

While an enterprise approach to IT services is a positive step in and of itself, it has the added advantage of providing the interagency IT infrastructure to support shared personnel, financial management, and other mission support services.

The federal government has already taken steps in this direction, beginning with the Bush administration's Lines of Business initiative (LOB), under which federal organizations provide administrative services such as payroll, personnel action processing, and basic accounting for a fee to other agencies.

But the original promise of this shared-services initiative has not been fully met. The vision was that shared-service providers would assume even more of the government's common administrative workload, including labor-intensive functions, such as the interaction between the manager and the personnel specialist before a promotion decision is made and processed.

Now is the time to realize that promise by having the administration more aggressively seek enterprise efficiencies.

8) Adopt an Enterprise Approach to the Acquisition of Goods and Services

Historically, the federal government has taken a decentralized, agency-centric approach to buying goods that practically every organization needs. In short, the government has not taken full advantage of its collective purchasing power to get the best deals for the taxpayer.

Here is a graphic example: Buying individually, agencies spend more than $500 million a year on cleaning products through nearly 4,000 contracts with 1,200 vendors. One agency paid $32 per case of paper towels, while another paid $61 for the exact same product.

Both the Bush and Obama administrations have sought to take a more strategic approach by leveraging the federal government's buying power. But this has largely been focused on consolidating acquisition strategies and contracts at the department level rather than across the federal enterprise.

That is why the Office of Federal Procurement Policy (OFPP) and the General Services Administration (GSA) should rapidly expand the scope of enterprise strategic sourcing, employing goal leaders, portfolios, and crosscutting accountability.

9) Build an Enterprise Civil-Service System

Today's federal civil-service system is obsolete. Its major components were last retooled more than four decades ago, which means the civil service today reflects the needs and characteristics of the last century's government work and workforce, not those required for today's complex, interagency challenges.

A revitalized and revamped civil-service system should ensure that federal agencies can attract, motivate, and retain skilled, energized, and engaged employees who can be deployed where needed to support the enterprise without compromising core civil-service principles that have defined the American civil service since its inception—merit, political neutrality, veterans preference, due process, collective bargaining, and nondiscrimination.

Among other things, the civil service must embrace a common but modernized job-classification system to ensure generally equal pay for equal work across agencies and a common, market-based compensation system tied to that classification structure to ensure parity with the U.S. labor market.

Agencies also need to be given more discretion to tailor policies to fit their specific needs, allowing them under certain conditions to customize salary rates for mission-critical occupations and to develop their own unique promotion and career patterns, performance-management policies, and a host of other workplace practices.

Additionally, OPM should devise an enterprise strategic human-capital plan focused on recruiting the type of specialized expertise government is likely to need in the future, including people with expertise in cyber-security, science, technology, engineering, and math.

For more information on the *Building the Enterprise* report, visit *www.ourpublicservice.org/OPS/publications/viewcontentdetails.php?id=228*

MAKE GOVERNMENT WORK!

Also in 2013, No Labels released our *Make Government Work!* action plan. Unlike the two plans outlined above, this one relies exclusively on new legislation. But the proposed bills in *Make Government Work!* were specifically designed to attract bipartisan support, and every one has been introduced in the House or Senate with bipartisan cosponsors. Now, the challenge is to turn them into law.

Make Government Work! has some overlapping ideas and concepts with both *Make Congress Work!* and *Building the Enterprise*. We have nonetheless placed the full menu of *Make Government Work!* proposals below, along with the relevant bill numbers and congressional cosponsors.

1) No Budget, No Pay
See earlier proposal in Make Congress Work! This idea would tie congressional pay to timely passage of budget and spending bills.

Lead Sponsors: Sen. Dean Heller (R-NV)

and Rep. Jim Cooper (D-TN)
Bill Numbers: S. 124 and H.R. 310

2) Take the Time, Save the Dime

There are many reasons for America's dire fiscal condition. There is, of course, the simple matter of what government spends—too much. But there is also the matter of how we spend it.

Even if budgets are passed on time, the budget process itself is still an unwieldy, all-consuming exercise—crowding out other legislative business and leaving too little time for Congress to engage in effective oversight.

In other words, Congress spends way too much time figuring out how to spend taxpayer money instead of figuring out if that money is being put to good use.

Congress should establish a two-year "biennial" budgeting cycle for the U.S. government, which would enable members to focus more on long-term strategic planning.

Under this new biennial budgeting process, Congress would complete its budget resolution and appropriations bills in the first year of each Congress and conduct an oversight and review process in the second year.

Lead Sponsors: Sen. Angus King (I-ME) and
Rep. Reid Ribble (R-WI)
Lead Co-Sponsor: Rep. Kurt Schrader (D-OR)
Bill Numbers: S. 554, H.R. 1869

3) Don't Duplicate, Consolidate

As noted in the *Building the Enterprise Report*, too many federal programs are fragmented (different entities handling little parts of big problems), overlapping (different entities handling similar problems), or duplicative (different entities handling the same problems).

The GAO's 2013 report made 300 different recommendations to reduce duplication and inefficiency in government, but

Congress and the Obama administration still have not addressed about 30 percent of those.

Each federal agency should begin working immediately to implement GAO's recommendations and should be required to report to Congress within six months the specific actions that have or will be taken by the executive branch and detail any actions that need to be authorized by Congress.

Lead Sponsors: Sen. Joe Manchin (D-WV)
and Rep. Charlie Dent (R-PA)
Lead Co-Sponsors: Sen. Kelly Ayotte (R-NH)
and Rep. Patrick Murphy (D-FL)
Bill Numbers: S. 1231, H.R. 2506

4) Buy Smarter, Save More

Also noted in the *Building the Enterprise Report* is the fact that much of the federal government's $500 billion in annual procurement spending is fragmented and uncoordinated.

For this reason, Congress should direct OMB to require all federal agencies to identify products and services that can be strategically sourced and set a mandate for at least $100 billion worth of annual purchases using this approach. Each cabinet-level department should have a senior dedicated strategic sourcing officer to ensure that it is indeed buying smarter and saving taxpayers more.

Based on data from other large organizations that have committed to strategic sourcing and on estimates from experts, this proposal could save the federal government at least $10 billion per year.

Lead Sponsors: Sen. Mark Begich (D-AK)
and Rep. Tim Griffin (R-AR)
Lead Co-Sponsors: Reps. Dan Maffei (D-NY),
Tom Reed (R-NY), Todd Young (R-IN)
Bill Numbers: S. 1304, H.R. 2694

5) No Adding, No Padding

Too much of government spending is on autopilot.

Congress and federal agencies rely on a variety of budgetary procedures that together conspire to effectively put increases in year-to-year government spending on autopilot. A leading culprit is the automatic use of inflation adjustments to increase federal agency budgets before proposals are submitted to Congress each year.

Congress should direct OMB to remove inflation as a factor in determining annual agency budgets.

Nothing in this law would prevent Congress from appropriating whatever it wants to fund a government agency or program. But it would force every federal agency to justify increases in its budget based on the merits and needs of their programs instead of merely assuming automatic inflation-adjusted increases in year-to-year funding.

Lead Sponsors: Sen. Amy Klobuchar (D-MN)
and Rep. Kurt Schrader (D-OR)
Lead Co-Sponsors: Sen. Kelly Ayotte (R-NH)
and Rep. Tom Reed (R-NY)
Bill Numbers: S. 1321, H.R. 2686

6) 21st Century Health Care for Heroes

Americans were outraged when they learned that hundreds of thousands of U.S. military veterans were waiting months or even years to get access to medical benefits through the Department of Veterans Affairs (VA).[204] The revelation was a reminder that our troops—many of them veterans of the wars in Iraq and Afghanistan—are often not getting the care they deserve.

But the VA backlog isn't the only problem with our military health-care system. Another glaring problem is that the Department of Defense (DOD) and the VA still don't have a unified system of electronic health records. Because DOD handles medical care for active duty servicemen and women and

---

204 www.veteransforcommonsense.org/

VA handles care for veterans, this poses a particular challenge for troops transitioning between military and civilian life.

That is why Congress should mandate full interoperability of DOD and VA medical records in the very near future. Congress and the executive branch have been directing these two agencies to merge military medical records for the better part of a decade—but the stark reality is that it just has not happened yet.

Lead Sponsors: Sen. Bill Nelson (D-FL)
and Rep. Chris Gibson (R-NY)
Lead Co-Sponsors: Reps. Ami Bera (D-CA),
Paul Cook (R-CA), Raul Ruiz (D-CA)
Bill Numbers: S. 1296, H.R. 2590

UPDATE: A version of this bill was included in the FY2014 Consolidated Appropriations Act and signed into law in January 2014.

7) Stay in Place, Cut the Waste

Every day, federal employees shuttle across the country and the world for conferences, training programs, business meetings, court and administrative hearings, and more. These travel expenses cost the federal government billions of dollars a year.

Some of this travel is essential but much of it is not, especially with the advent of more affordable and accessible video conferencing and other teleworking technology. Many businesses and other large organizations are taking full advantage of this technological revolution, but the federal government has lagged far behind.

Congress should direct the Office of Management and Budget (OMB) to review existing agency efforts to cut travel costs and to submit a plan to Congress to achieve an additional 50 percent cut in future travel by replacing it with video conferencing.

This is an ambitious goal that could save American taxpayers billions of dollars.

Lead Sponsor: Rep. Mike Fitzpatrick (R-PA)
Lead Co-Sponsor: Rep. John Barrow (D-GA)
Bill Number: H.R. 2642

8) Wasted Energy, Wasted Dollars

America wastes more energy than any other developed country.

Because the federal government is America's largest energy consumer, it has a critical role to play in charting our nation's path toward greater energy efficiency.

To save taxpayer dollars by making federal buildings more energy efficient, the administration should implement more energy-conservation measures, including public-private partnerships like Energy Savings Performance Contracts (ESPCs), which achieve savings at no up-front cost to taxpayers. Companies performing ESPC work secure their own financing to design and implement energy efficiency projects, and they are then paid out of savings achieved by their work. If the savings are not realized, the contractor is not paid.

Lead Sponsors: Reps. Cory Gardner (R-CO)
and Peter Welch (D-VT)
Bill Number: S. 1308, H.R. 2689

9) Plan for Efficient and Effective Government

Every year think tanks, auditors, investigators, and even Uncle Sam's own Government Accountability Office crank out report after report concluding the same thing:

Too many federal government programs are inefficient, costly, ineffective, or all of the above.

And yet every year these conclusions are largely ignored.

It's time for a more rigorous focus on what government does, how it does it, how it performs, how we pay for it, and how we measure success.

Congress should pass a law creating a new bipartisan Commission for Government Transformation, which would oversee and affect the transformation of various federal government programs and functions so they will be more economical, efficient, and effective.

The commission would feature seven members—appointed by the president and the leadership of both parties in the House and the Senate—and a dedicated expert staff that would review all activities of government and develop specific recommendations for the White House and Congress.

Lead Sponsors: Sen. Mark Kirk (R-IL)
and Rep. Cheri Bustos (D-IL)
Lead Co-Sponsors: Reps. Sean Duffy (R-WI),
David Cicilline (D-RI) and Mike Fitzpatrick (R-PA)
Bill Number: S. 1297, H.R. 2675

For more information on the *Make Government Work!* action plan, visit *www.nolabels.org/make-government-work*

A Better Congress. A Better Government. A Better Chance To Achieve the National Strategic Agenda

The ideas featured in this chapter don't address the hot-button issues that are typically the subject of partisan sparring on cable TV.

But these proposals are absolutely essential to a better-functioning Congress and federal government. They address the nitty-gritty governance issues that are too often ignored in the debates about big ideas. And No Labels believes that you simply can't address jobs, Social Security and Medicare, the budget, or energy without also improving the performance of the institutions that make and carry out our laws.

Although many of these proposals address arcane procedures and practices of our government, that does not mean they will be easy to implement. Make no mistake: These ideas are a threat to the status quo, and those who benefit from the status quo will resist reform efforts.

But No Labels has worked to identify proposals that stand a realistic shot at success.

For example, *Make Congress Work!* and *Building the Enterprise* rely primarily on ideas that can be executed with simple rule or behavioral changes in Congress or executive and administrative actions that build on previous government reform initiatives.

Meanwhile, every proposal in *Make Government Work!* can claim broad bipartisan support and co-sponsorship.

That's no guarantee that these promising ideas will become policy. But it certainly increases the odds.

As with all the ideas in the *National Strategic Agenda*, these ideas must be embraced and pushed by citizens across the country who make clear to their leaders that a better-functioning Congress and government are priorities that demand urgent attention.

OUR CALL TO ACTION: MAKING THE NATIONAL STRATEGIC AGENDA A REALITY

It's Up to All of Us

We know the task ahead won't be easy.

Washington has grown so dysfunctional that many Americans have turned off and tuned out. They're convinced their voices won't be heard and they've given up hope that our leaders can ever find a way to break through the gridlock.

But we can't afford to give up.

As we've illustrated in this book, too much is at stake. This isn't just about America's prosperity, security, and place in the world. It's also about the prosperity and security of millions of individual Americans and their families who will inevitably pay the price if Washington doesn't get its act together.

No Labels believes it is possible for our leaders to break the gridlock and get things done if they can come together over big ideas and achievable shared goals. That's how our country has always solved big problems in the past. And that's how the *National Strategic Agenda* aims to deal with our problems in the near future.

We have identified goals that most Americans recognize as urgent priorities. These are the challenges that common sense and basic arithmetic tell us have to be met in order for our nation to thrive and prosper in the decades ahead. We need:

- To create 25 million jobs that lift up families and match

the needs of our twenty-first-century economy.

- To secure Medicare and Social Security for this generation and generations to come.
- To balance the budget to keep our debt from overwhelming our economy and preventing us from investing in our future.
- To achieve real energy security by developing more abundant, affordable and sustainable forms of energy and by more efficiently using and distributing all the energy we have.

Throughout this book, we've articulated some general approaches and principles and outlined specific policies that can help achieve these goals. Though each of these four challenges must be examined one by one, they are all connected, interrelated, and integral parts of the total picture. As we've said throughout this book, fixing one of the problems will make it easier to fix the rest.

If we enact a smarter immigration policy, for instance, we can expand our labor force and enhance our pool of high-skilled talent, which leads to the potential for greater innovation and ultimately more jobs. But we can also expand the number of workers paying into safety-net programs at a time when we desperately need more revenues to pay for increasing numbers of beneficiaries. Easing these entitlement burdens, in turn, goes a long way toward helping us bring balance to the budget and putting us on sounder economic footing.

We're confident that once our political leaders summon the will to tackle even one of these challenges, they will recognize the need to deal with all of them holistically.

But the only way this will happen—the only way our elected officials will take up this challenge—is if we as citizens put pressure on them to do so.

It's up to us now to light a fire under our leaders in Washington and to make clear to them that a *National Strategic Agenda* is a top priority for the citizens of this country, that we expect them to commit to this concept of progress through shared goals—and that we will hold them accountable if they don't.

In the next year, there will be plenty of opportunities for citizens to help learn about, shape, and build support for this agenda. No Labels has already scheduled events in Washington, DC, New Hampshire, Iowa, and elsewhere beginning in the fall of 2014 and continuing into 2015.

During that time, we'll be taking the pulse of federal, state, and local government leaders and of regular citizens to forge agreement on a full policy plan to achieve the goals of the *National Strategic Agenda*. The effort will culminate on October 5, 2015, when the fully formed *National Strategic Agenda* will be unveiled in New Hampshire during the height of the presidential election season. No Labels will work to inject the agenda into the emerging presidential debate by activating our network of citizens, members of Congress, and state and local leaders across New Hampshire and ultimately across America.

In the meantime, citizens can contact their representatives in Washington—via phone, e-mail, or social media—and ask if they support No Labels' call for a *National Strategic Agenda*. Applaud them if they say yes. If they say no, ask them why not and tell them it's critically important to you that they get behind this shared vision for our country. Do the same with any candidate for office—for the House and Senate, and, as we head to 2016, the presidency.

Our political leaders need to understand that the citizens of this country are fed up with partisan games and gridlock and a do-nothing government. We want a clear direction and a clear destination, and there needs to be a price to pay at the ballot box if leaders ignore this call to action.

We don't want the ideas outlined in this book to remain mere theories or intellectual exercises, joining scores of other thoughtful white papers and commission reports that collect dust in desk drawers and computer files all over the nation's capital. Through discussions, debates, working groups, negotiations, and good-faith, across-the-aisle problem solving, these goals and ideas need to be molded into specific policy proposals. They need to be turned into action. And they can be.

This is no time to let your frustration with the political process lead to disengagement and disillusionment.

Because America is facing a stark choice.

We can keep following the same unsuccessful hyper-partisan playbook that we've been following for much of the last decade.

The consequences of continuing down that path are clear, as the United States will be consigned to a future where unemployment is rising and incomes are dropping; where red ink overwhelms our budget and shreds our social safety net; and where our energy destiny is dictated by forces beyond our control.

Or we can choose a different path. Our leaders can come together as they have so many times in the past to develop a shared vision and achieve shared goals that will set our country on a sustainable, responsible, and prosperous path.

It's up to us—the American people—to show our elected leaders the way and to ensure that they hear this call for a *National Strategic Agenda* loud and clear.

ACKNOWLEDGMENTS

Just the Facts was created with input from a number of political and policy experts from across the political spectrum. No Labels would like to give special thanks to:

Rob Atkinson, Information Technology &
    Innovative Foundation
Admiral Dennis Blair
Aryeh Bourkoff, LionTree
Steve Case, Revolution
Jonathan Crane, Coalition for Evidence-Based Policy
John Dearie, Financial Services Forum
Charley Ebinger, Brookings Institution
Bill Galston, Brookings Institution
Courtney Geduldig, Standard & Poor's
David Goldwyn, Goldwyn Global Strategies
Chris Jennings, Jennings Policy Strategies
Rob Kaplan, Harvard Business School
Joe Kennedy, Information Technology and
    Innovation Foundation
Charlie Kolb, French-American Foundation
Michael Levi, Council on Foreign Relations
Dana Marshall, Transnational Strategy Group
Will Marshall, Progressive Policy Institute
Lenny Mendonca, McKinsey & Company
Jim Millstein, Millstein & Company
Clarine Nardi Riddle, Kasowitz, Benson,
    Torres & Friedman
Jim Nussle, The Nussle Group
Greg Pellegrino, Deloitte
Jim Pinkerton, New America Foundation

Alice Rivlin, Brookings Institution
Rob Shapiro, Sonecon
Max Stier, Partnership for Public Service
Michael Strain, The American Enterprise Institute
Marty Sullivan, Tax Analysts
Michael Udell, District Economics Group
Michael Useem, Wharton Business School
Staci Warden, Milken Institute

CONNECT WITH
NO LABELS

If you believe it's time for our leaders to start coming together around a *National Strategic Agenda*, then please get in touch and join our campaign. This is your movement—and we need your help to change politics for good.

**Sign up to join the movement at
www.NoLabels.org**

 **@NoLabelsOrg**

 **www.Facebook.com/NoLabels**

CPSIA information can be obtained at www.ICGtesting.com
Printed in the USA
BVOW11s2154030914

365400BV00004B/13/P

9 781626 814271